Praise for
The Mental Edge for Young Athletes

"Young athletes will connect with the insights in this book immediately. The parent guide is a fantastic addition, making *The Mental Edge for Young Athletes* a real contribution to the field."

— JAMES E. LOEHR, renowned performance psychologist and author of *New York Times* bestseller *The Power of Full Engagement*

"The depth of insight in this book will help young athletes master themselves while reaching their highest level of performance."

— DUANE KUIPER, sports announcer for the San Francisco Giants/ former professional baseball player

"As a parent of three competitive athletes, I wish I had access to the wisdom you will find in this remarkable guide. Jeff Greenwald's vast experience in this crucial aspect of performance will touch you on every page."

— GRAHAM WEAVER, founder and CEO of Alpine Investors; lecturer, Stanford Graduate School of Business

"As an elite athlete on the Masters Tour, Jeff's real-life experience and expertise in the field will give your child a huge step forward in reaching their potential."

— BRAD GILBERT, author of *Winning Ugly: Mental Warfare in Tennis— Lessons from a Master*, former World No. 4 on the ATP Tour

"Jeff's wealth of knowledge based on research, his own experience as a professional tennis player, and work with hundreds of teenage athletes and parents will help you enjoy competition, experience less stress, and win more. What could be better than that?"

— CRAIG NELSON, chairman of the board, Nelson Staffing

"Empathy and knowledge, insight and ideas—these are the cornerstones of Jeff Greenwald's remarkable mind and generous heart. With clarity and kindness, this engaging book provides an excellent blueprint for navigating the tricky waters of competition."

—JOEL DRUCKER, tennis historian/USTA NorCal
Hall of Fame inductee

"Jeff's book is in the same zip code as *Mamba Mentality*—pure gold. He's taken the brutal, real-life lessons we stumble through face-first and turned them into gripping and straight-up cinematic stuff. Reading this feels like watching a movie in my brain—like a documentary I didn't know I needed. *The Mental Edge for Young Athletes* has just dethroned every other high-level mindset book out there. That's how good it is."

—COACH JEROME GUMBS, founder of the Empower Me Academy

"If you want to be an exceptional athlete and an extraordinary human being, read *The Mental Edge for Young Athletes*. Sports are so much more than competition, fun and games: They are a vehicle to a better life. Doubling down on the mental-toughness skills and healthy habits built into the journey of becoming an athlete will help you grow into the most remarkable version of you. Consider *The Mental Edge for Young Athletes* as your road map to victory as an athlete and Olympic gold as a human being."

—SHEILA OHLSSON WALKER, PHD, author of *Wise Decisions:*
A Science-Based Approach to Making Better Choices

"In *The Mental Edge for Young Athletes*, Jeff successfully highlights the most important elements that will help athletes excel in their sport. I recommend this book to any young athlete and for those parents wanting to get the most out of their sports experience."

—CHARLES SCOTT, founder of Future Prospects and former professional baseball player

The

Mental Edge for Young Athletes

A World Champion's Mental Toughness Guide for Athletes, Parents, and Coaches in the Digital Age

Jeff Greenwald, MFT
Two-Time World Champion

ISBN: 979-8-9926109-1-8 Paperback
ISBN: 979-8-9926109-2-5 Ebook

To my loving parents
Howard and Marilynn Greenwald
*for your unwavering support and endless generosity from the
moment I declared my quest to become a professional athlete
at the age of twelve. Thank you for your loving support.*

A special dedication to my remarkable children
Ally and Will
*who continue to challenge and impress me in so many
ways. You will always be my most cherished gifts.*

*And to all of my young athletes and their families for
trusting me and having the courage to do the hard work.
Your commitment to mastery inspired me to write this book.*

With love and gratitude,
Jeff

Contents

Introduction

HAVE YOU EVER FELT like you were on fire in practice, then stepped into competition and felt it all fly out the window?

Or maybe it wasn't a total disaster, just a slow breakdown: Your legs felt like they were stuck in cement, your mind started spinning, and suddenly it felt as though someone else was controlling your body. No matter how much you tried to fix it, it only got worse.

Welcome to the mental game.

When I was twelve, my parents sent me to a tennis academy (more like a boot camp with guards!) with eighty other obsessed tennis players from all over the globe—each dreaming of becoming a pro. We learned how to hit the ball really hard and ran around swamps with alligators in one-hundred-degree heat to get physically fit. But coaches never talked about what to do when we got tight and nervous, which happened all the time. They didn't give us any tools to manage mistakes and our fear of losing. It took many years to realize that something important was missing from our training. Of course, now there is an excellent mental toughness program in place to help athletes develop these crucial skills.

But it's hard to believe that by fifteen, despite competing at a high level in multiple sports, I had no clue that the chatter in my head had anything to do with my performance or the outcome of the match. It never occurred to me that there might be a way to control the nervous energy surging through my body. If only I had realized that managing mistakes was up to me. My coaches told me I was a hothead, but I had a hard time applying what they told me—until I was banned from competing, which you'll soon hear about.

But now everyone seems to be talking about this aspect of sports—the mental game. The mental what? When I was a teenage athlete, other than one short visit to a hypnotist (yes, my mother was that desperate for me to get a handle on my anger), I had no idea what this mental game thing was about.

I just never learned how to control my intense frustration in competition—like the time I slammed my baseball bat against the fence or when I missed a routine shot on a big point in a tennis match. If only someone had given me the statistics—that getting just three out of ten hits in the Major Leagues will land a player in the Hall of Fame. Or that the world's number one tennis player only wins approximately 55 percent of the points? Seriously? Winning a little more than half of the points in a tennis match, and I would be ranked number one in the world? I hope you let that sink in. Even at a young age, knowing these statistics would have stopped me in my tracks. The takeaway: Being perfect is unnecessary and not the right mindset.

Given that I knew virtually nothing about the mental aspect when I was your age, maybe you can understand why I occasionally wish I could travel back in time. I would give anything for the opportunity to hand my younger self every single one of the principles in this book. It would have changed the course of my career. Perhaps with AI, a virtual journey back in time will one day become a reality!

Even better, though, I thought, *"What if I could teach others—young athletes like you—how to master your mind while you're still in your prime and dealing with a ton of stress? How meaningful,"* I imagined, *"it would be to help you maximize your ability with the same strategies and tools that I've been teaching athletes like yourself for the past twenty-five years."*

But then the fear began to trickle in nearly every day. *"Jeff, teenagers don't read anymore unless it's for school. How can you compete with TikTok and Instagram? You're wasting your time."*

I was falling into the same trap you probably face all the time: wanting an outcome that you can't fully control—in my case, to write a book that you would read—but doubting I could do it.

I decided that my only chance of success would be to help you overcome the number one mental barrier in sports—fear. Fear of mistakes. Fear of losing. Fear of the things you think people will say if you lose. Fear of being tight. Fear, even, of fear.

If you decide to join me on this path of mastery, I can promise you won't be disappointed. But, it will also be challenging. I say this because you are flooded with messages about winning and losing all day long. Maybe your parents get caught in it, too. We must be aware if we are going to win this war for a mastery mindset, which you will soon learn about. Don't think for a second that the innocent, post-match questions "Did you win?" or "How did you do?" aren't taking over your mind. They are.

These questions don't even include the highlight reels in the news or selected posts on social media that isolate and glorify the less than .01 percent of the population at the top of their sport. "Making it big" (winning money, achieving status, and finding fame) seems normal and almost expected when we see this at any time of the day. Statistics also show that over 30 percent of kids your age suffer from general anxiety. This means that one out of every three of your classmates is feeling worried and uptight nearly all the time.

Listen, I'm not saying you will become mentally tough overnight. But if you embrace the principles in this book and commit to putting them into action when you compete, there is no question you will get better and win a lot more. You will learn how to maintain your focus for longer stretches. You will be able to refocus when distractions come up, you will feel looser under pressure while still keeping your intensity high, and you will never give up.

By staying curious and being willing to explore the well-tested strategies in this book, I'm confident you can bridge the gap between practice and competition, just like countless athletes around the world are doing today. Remember, becoming more aware of how you show up under pressure isn't a weakness. It is a crucial factor to achieve success at every level of sport.

Everything you will read in this book is supported by solid research and real-life examples from the greatest athletes across the globe. You will find personal stories from my experience as a youth athlete, a Division 1 (D1) college player, and a professional tennis player, alongside important insights that emerged from honest conversations over two decades with young athletes just like you. My young clients all learned the lessons I will share with you that moved them closer to the best performances of their lives.

In her Netflix documentary, Simone Biles shared, "I would have quit five hundred times if it hadn't been for my teammates, who kept encouraging me to come back to the gym. They've meant everything to me. I see a therapist now, and it's helping me understand everything that's happening."

I have one favor to ask: I need your curiosity and engagement throughout this book. I've made the chapters relatively short and practical for this reason. You simply won't develop this mental edge without having your own motivation to learn. I know you have a lot going on in your life. I also realize that my greatest challenge is to keep your attention here long enough so you can learn some of these principles and then apply them in competition.

I know that even if these strategies sound interesting to you as you read, your brain will want to pull you back to those funny videos on TikTok. I don't believe that I am competing with the homework you have to do. Maintaining your focus is going to be a battle between the quick hits you get from your Snaps, TikTok videos, and Instagram photos, and your willingness to take the time to work on this part of your game. If you come with me on this ride, I am confident that you will improve dramatically. You will find a new dimension of focus and mastery that surprises you.

As you absorb the lessons and tools in this book, please take your time and don't rush through the pages. I wrote this book so you can pick a chapter to read based on how you're feeling and what you're facing on any given day. There is also a companion workbook (you can download or purchase with the QR code in this book) that will guide you through specific exercises and reflective questions to deepen your learning so you can apply these strategies in real-time. This will be a great asset in making sure you translate these skills into competition.

Remember, you are the ultimate judge of your progress. Set an intention each day to work on these tools and principles in practice, and by the end of this book, you will be holding your own personal remote control in your hand. It is the key to an upward spiral of success that you are about to unlock. It's what I did, what all successful professional athletes have learned to do, and what you will also be doing.

SECTION 1

Mindset & Motivation

WHY DO SOME ATHLETES keep improving while others plateau or burn out?

It often comes down to how they think—about progress, pressure, and purpose. In this section, you'll shift away from perfectionism and outcome obsession toward a deeper, more durable kind of motivation.

These chapters will help you adopt a growth mindset, handle challenges without spiraling, and find meaning in the process—even when results are slow to come. If you want to thrive in sports and beyond, it starts with how you see yourself as a learner and competitor.

In this section, you'll learn how to:
- Let go of rigid expectations and judgments.
- Find joy in improvement, not just results.
- Fuel your progress with curiosity and purpose.

1

Build a Mastery Mindset

"THERE IS NO WAY," I scream, for the third time after missing another easy shot. It's the finals of a junior tournament at the infamous Nick Bollettieri Tennis Academy (now IMG Academy), and I can't control my anger anymore. In that moment, the referee in the chair looks down at me and says, "Unsportsman-like conduct. Game, set, and match." Meaning: I'm disqualified—basically, I'm thrown out of the match for bad behavior. But that isn't the end of it. The referee then comes down from the chair and delivers the hammer: "And I'm also banning you from tournaments in the Florida Tennis Association." I'm too stunned to respond. I'm angry and embarrassed. But there's nothing I can do. It's over.

I remember being in total shock at the idea of not being able to compete anymore. I loved competing even if it made me crazy sometimes.

But often we get a second chance if we take responsibility for our actions. That's exactly what I did. With the help of one of the coaches at the academy, I wrote a letter to the tennis association, apologized for my behavior, and assured them it wouldn't happen again. They agreed to place me on probation, and I was allowed to play tournaments again the following month. I did calm down a good amount—I had to if I still wanted to compete—but I still needed a ton of help with my mental game.

At the time, I just wanted to win. No, I *had* to win. The thought of losing freaked me out. I didn't know what the mental game was—how to think about competition or what to do when I got tight. I had no idea that I could shift my focus when I wanted to. I was just hoping to play well and win, and not come up short and lose. I didn't know how different these two perspectives were—playing to win versus playing not to lose. But they are very different, and each approach will have a huge impact on the outcome.

Even though I did earn a scholarship to UC Santa Barbara, a D1 university, and played a few years of professional tennis afterward, this tug-of-war between my need to win and my fear of losing describes most of my young career as an athlete.

However, after I left the pro tour, I ended up playing for a club in Germany. It was there that I stumbled upon something simple but magical, at which point everything changed. I realized that when I chose to direct my attention—like, *all of it*—on specific, productive things in the moment, I felt more confident. I also began winning more—much more. This discovery led me to a much deeper understanding of the concept of *mastery*—an entirely new mindset that helps us focus on what we control in the *present* instead of worrying about what might happen in the future.

This *mastery* mindset is exactly what helped Michael Jordan, believed to be the greatest basketball player of all time, famously rise from the ashes of failure when he was cut from his varsity high school team as a sophomore but who, with determination and effort, went on to win the NCAA Championship at the University of North Carolina, Chapel Hill, and snag six NBA titles in his pro career.

He said, "I can accept failure. Everyone fails at something. But I can't accept not trying. . . . I've missed more than nine thousand shots in my career. I've lost almost three hundred games. Twenty-six times, I've been trusted to take the game-winning shot and missed. I've failed over and over again in my life. And that is why I succeed."

But here's the thing. When you're older and have already achieved some legit success on the big stage, isn't it easy to say that the failures were necessary and part of the success? These athletes have no doubt that success will eventually come—because it already did! What about those of us who haven't achieved similar success yet? How are we supposed to remain confident after hard losses with only occasional signs of success, at best?

Well, it requires a lot of faith, a good dose of patience, and maybe a little logic. Success doesn't happen overnight. You know that. It's getting past the emotional pain of a bad performance or disappointing loss that is our greatest challenge. All successful athletes feel this burning pain from losing because they care so deeply about what they're doing. But despite this pain and disappointment, they don't give up when they hit a bump in the road. They dig deep because they have developed a mastery mindset. They are always looking for ways to improve.

Barry Bonds, a former San Francisco Giant and one of baseball's most dominant hitters, whose mental focus and poise under pressure offer a powerful example for any athlete, once called the constant intentional walks "probably the hardest thing I've gone through in my career. But I had the mentality and the focus to withstand it." That season, pitchers denied him the strike zone—and he responded with mental discipline instead of frustration. Four days after losing his father, he came back to hit a walk-off homer. Through grief, raw emotion, and pressure, he stayed present. That's mental toughness in action.

It's important to understand that the more painful the loss, the more you will learn. I know these losses can sting badly. It may take a few days to pull that stinger out. But when you refocus on improving your skills for the future and maintain a mastery mindset, I guarantee you will play better and achieve more than you can even imagine right now.

Doesn't it make sense that you're going to lose for a while— some big games and important events—learn from them, and eventually translate these lessons into future competition? Of course, it's tough emotionally, but it is also reasonable. And, because every successful athlete goes through this cycle, it is wise to accept that it's true: Failure leads to success. This approach is how you build mental toughness. You also have nothing to lose with this mindset and everything to gain.

If a coach had helped me realize that it wasn't the loss that would determine my future, but rather how I reacted to that loss, would it have made a difference in how I handled losing? Definitely. Especially if they taught me how to build this mindset—the same mindset you will develop if you stay locked in with me through this book.

How much do you worry about an event that's coming up in a few days? How are you supposed to not get sucked into this whirlpool of fear—fear of not performing well, disappointing your coach, or losing another heartbreaking game?

Let's take a closer look at this situation. It's a big event. You really want to win. It's what your parents, teammates, and coaches are all talking about. But wait. Let's hit the pause button. This is where things can take a wrong turn when you get caught in thinking about what might happen or what you feel should happen. But the outcome and how well you play are never 100 percent certain. While not knowing the outcome seems like it's the problem—the reason you are worrying about it—it's actually what makes competition so exciting. Think about this for a moment longer. Uncertainty is the very thing that creates the element of tension and surprise. Being aware of this principle is a big deal and a tremendous opportunity for you right now. You can learn to embrace uncertainty. Even though your survival-focused mind wasn't wired to like the unknown, you can begin to see the uncertainty of competition as part of the excitement.

Here's the thing—we can't control everything. We can't guarantee a win or make ourselves play amazing every time. But you want some proof that it will go well, don't you? You want something. Some sign. Some feeling. Confidence would definitely help, but maybe yours is low right now. What are you supposed to do? What about all of those anxious thoughts swirling around in your head?

Sometimes people might try to take the pressure off you. For instance, just before you go into the game, they tell you to "just have fun." But does this last-second pre-game prompt take the pressure off you? No. It's too big of a stretch. When you hear that, it might even feel like more pressure to you. You're probably thinking, *"Yeah, I'll have fun as long as I play well and we win."*

Of course, you want to have fun and play well, but you mostly want to win. You know that winning is what most people seem to care about—like whether you are on the varsity team or where you'll go to college—and that it influences how your team-mates, friends, coach, and parents think about you.

While it is true that reminding yourself to have fun can help you relax and play better, it's the commitment to the things within the *mastery mindset*—playing with intention, giving yourself permission to miss, executing your tactics, embracing both the challenge and your nerves—that will become your best pre-game mentality. It is the mastery mindset that will help you play your best and win.

Your opportunity now is to get excited about something we call "the process"—executing the strategies and using the tools that will lead you to your best performance. Athletes and coaches often refer to this as "controlling the controllables," the number-one goal of every accomplished athlete.

But you might ask: *"What about the people constantly talking about who won and who lost?"* Let them. You can't control what others think or do.

Anyone talking about outcome so frequently simply doesn't yet understand the powerful secret of the mastery mindset that you will be building. As you approach competition from this mindset, you will notice these outcome-based conversations even more. This is good. It means you are becoming more aware of this trap. This will be your challenge and fight every single day—to focus on mastery and letting the outcome take care of itself.

Just a few days ago, a thirteen-year-old baseball player told me about his frustration with people talking about winning and losing but nothing else: "Lately, after every game, my friends ask me if we won or lost. If I say we won, but it was close, they say, 'It was that close?' If I say we lost, they respond, 'Oh, I thought you would definitely win that one.' What am I supposed to do?" he asked in frustration. "I always leave the conversation feeling bad. It never ends."

Is it a surprise that we get so tight in competition? How often do people ask if you won or lost after practice? Other than your coach or maybe your parents, probably no one. I want you to be aware of the difference between mastery (process) and outcome so you can take more control of your mindset and your choices. You don't have to think exactly like everybody else. Be stubborn about your mental approach on game day. Have pride in your new mindset, especially when you commit to it under pressure. When you find yourself thinking, *"What if this happens? What if that happens?"* you can shift your focus back to what you have control over—how you choose to respond.

Over the years, I've worked with thousands of athletes who've struggled with this common habit of getting stuck in their heads, worrying about losing. In fact, I'm sharing a mindset worksheet on the next page because I want you to see why your skills just disappear out of nowhere.

Athletes love seeing the contrast between these two mindsets so concretely. They are surprised that there is a straight-forward way to develop a mastery mindset.

Take a look at the two columns on the next page. Do you see how the left column under mastery might lead to better performances?

Competing with a mastery mindset becomes a choice you get to make.

It's important to understand that you can care about both winning and mastery at the same time. It doesn't have to be one or the other. Ironically, when you lead with the mastery mindset, you will actually win more. This choice becomes more achievable when you become more aware of your thoughts and reactions. You will have a chance to self-reflect and apply this awareness

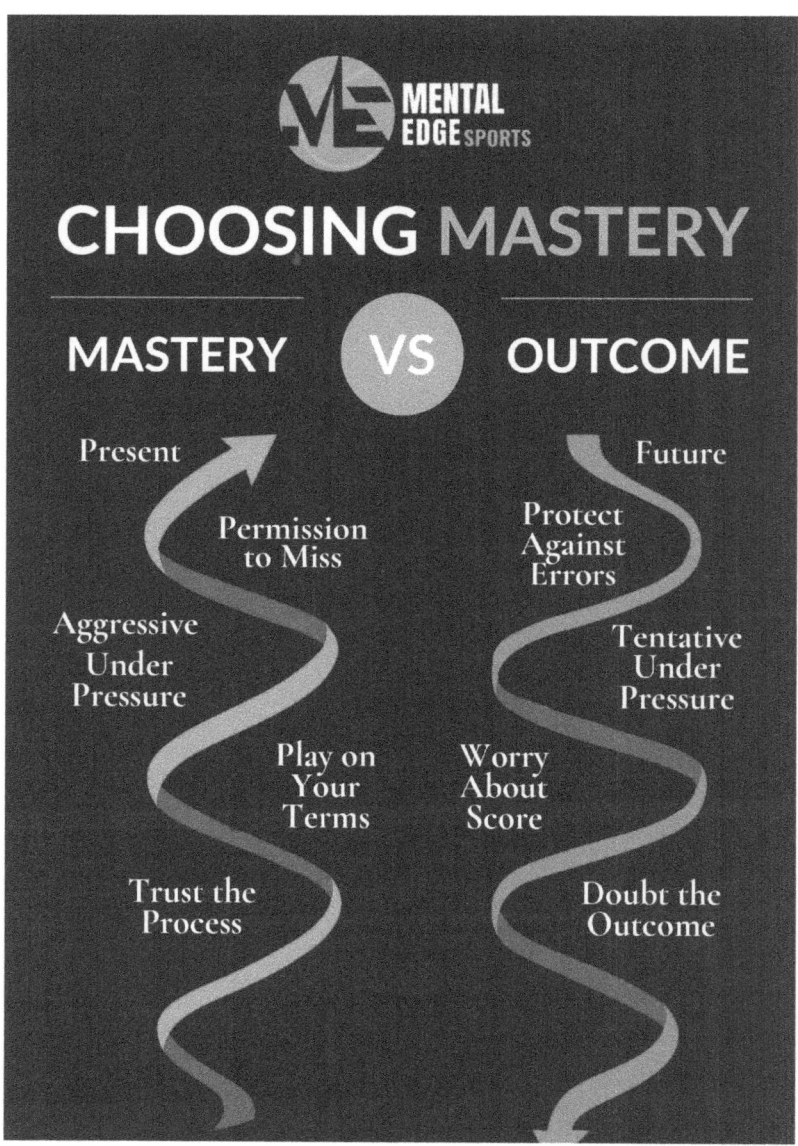

throughout this book, and with the help of my accompanying workbook, if you also have that.

To put the principles you learn into practice during challenging times, ask yourself a simple question: *"What's my mindset right now—mastery or outcome?"*

Consider this chapter as the foundation for the entire book. What comes next is the GPS that will help you execute the mastery mindset and win more—in this order. It's time for you to get the playbook so you can squeeze the most out of your ability and achieve your goals.

2

Be Curious and Seek Feedback

THE LATE AND GREAT Kobe Bryant, one of the best basketball players in history, knew the most important secret of all: Curiosity about what you're doing—if you want to get better—is the skill and quality that will move you to the top of your sport. At the very least, it will help you get the most out of your ability.

"Most players that play the game will just play it," Kobe told *The Athletic.* "Certain things will happen, some may be good, some may be bad. I don't know. That wasn't good enough for me. I want to know why. . . . I think it's that constant curiosity that will separate you."

Have you ever unlocked a new skill just by making a simple technical adjustment? For instance, your coach told you to do something a little differently, and suddenly everything just clicked?

Curiosity is kind of like that. It will open you up to a new dimension of learning and performance. It feels like a desire to feel something in a new way; a motivation to close the gap on what you don't know and what you want to know more about. In other words, by not backing down from challenges, you will feel better and have more success. That probably sounds like a bold statement. I'll double down and even make it my personal promise to you.

The truth is, it's inherently fun to be curious. It can be really satisfying to want to know *how* to do something differently or better. Being in a curious state triggers the release of dopamine—a brain chemical that creates excitement, as if you're getting a text message from someone you like at school. It's sort of like that.

When we drop into this state of wonder and tap into our natural human desire to know things or to solve a problem, we create even more interest, which feeds on itself and creates an upward spiral that will only bring you more success and satisfaction over time.

This concept may not make sense to you quite yet, especially in the context of sports. Sure, you're curious about whether you'll play well and win next weekend. But the kind of curiosity I'm describing isn't about the outcome—although the outcome usually ends up better because of it. It's about the desire to find a way to close the gap between where you are right now and where you want to be.

At first glance, maybe you think that being curious is either something you have or you don't. Clearly, there are obstacles that prevent you from being in a state of curiosity more often. It's not like every day at school, or even practice, is all that new and different. I'm also not bashing TikTok, but how much time do you even *have* to be curious about any of the videos you're seeing before the next one shows up?

But let's go back to the late Kobe. "When I was young," Kobe shared, "I didn't just want to play basketball; I wanted to understand it. I was curious about everything—the footwork, the techniques, and the mindsets of other successful players."

Kobe would watch tapes of Michael Jordan, Magic Johnson, and other legends of the game. He'd study their moves frame by frame. "I wanted to know what made them great," he explained. "Every time they made a play, I asked why. Why did they choose that move? What did they see?"

This curiosity led Kobe to seek advice from many people, not just basketball players. He talked with coaches, trainers, and athletes competing in other sports to learn how to get the most out of his training.

Kobe's curiosity wasn't just about on-court performance. He wanted to understand mental conditioning and how he could become a leader. "I realized that to be the best, I needed to explore all aspects of being an athlete. Curiosity opened doors to new strategies that I was able to add into my own game."

This constant curiosity fueled Kobe's legendary work ethic and commitment to improvement. It drove him to constantly refine his game, even in the face of challenges and after numerous victories.

"Curiosity," Kobe often reflected, "is what makes the journey exciting and fulfilling. It's the key to unlocking potential."

Kobe Bryant's story is just one example of how to use curiosity to your advantage. Let this impulse to know more, to understand yourself and your sport, drive you. It will propel you forward beyond anything you can imagine. It will also make the ride so much sweeter.

3

Let Go of Your Expectations

"Oh, YOU SHOULD BEAT *that team. You shouldn't have a problem beating her.*" If you aren't hearing it from other people, you're saying it to yourself. Have you noticed that anytime an opponent is considered to be weaker than you or your team, the word "should"—which I now call a six-letter swear word—has a way of automatically poisoning the conversation? This word does only one thing—it raises expectations and makes you feel anxious. Now, you are *supposed* to win. But with this outcome-based mindset, if you win, you only did what you were supposed to do. If you lose, it feels like a failure.

Let me be clear. Expectations for an outcome—what you have only *some* control over—is pretty much the kiss of death for performance. Expectations on things you have partial control over will only lead to frustration and disappointment when things don't go the way you think they "should." This mindset will only pull and distract you from what you need to do to win.

This past week, I was talking to a tennis player who has been in a horrible slump for the past six months. He was playing below his level and couldn't seem to break out of this frustrating cycle.

After two weeks of working with him, I didn't see any real improvement, which told me that his mindset was not where it needed to be.

"What do you think is holding you back?" I asked.

"Since I was ten, I've wanted to be a pro," he shared with me. "Now I'm seeing this possibility drift further and further away." His eyes turned to the ground, clearly ashamed.

"It's like you're stuck in this room over here," I acknowledged, "and you can't seem to get out."

"Yeah. Every time I make a mistake or miss shots that I know I can make, I lose all hope and motivation that I will ever get there."

This player is handcuffed by his big goal of being a professional tennis player. Anything short of progress toward this goal ignites fear and worry. As a result, even swinging through the ball becomes a battle when this hope and expectation are clouding the mind.

Once the expectations kick in—regardless of the source—and you feel you have to win, your performance will decline. So, the next time the "should" text message arrives in your mind, remember that this is just spam, smile to yourself, and delete it.

Consider nineteen-year-old Kylian Mbappé—a household name during the 2018 FIFA World Cup, who was leading the French national team to victory. Mbappé had a ton of expectations placed on him. Once coaches and the media saw his ability, the expectations mounted—everyone was saying how great he should become.

But, somehow, in the 2018 World Cup final against Croatia, he was able to erase these expectations. In the final minutes, with the eyes of the world upon him, Mbappé received the ball on the edge of the box, took a touch to control it, and fired a powerful low shot past the Croatian goalkeeper, into the bottom-right corner of the net, making him the first teenager since Pelé to score in a World Cup final, cementing his status as a rising star on the global stage. After the game, Mbappé said, "I've learned to never let external expectations distract me from my goals." He resolutely ignored the noise about what others expected him to accomplish.

You, too, can learn to direct your focus away from all of the external distractions and shift your full attention toward the task in front of you. To develop this skill, you first need to consciously let go of the expectations from yourself and from others.

Mbappé understood he had a choice. He listened to himself. That's what I want you to do, too—trust your skills and be selective about who you let influence you.

Mbappé committed to a different set of expectations: to work harder than anyone else and to remind himself of how fortunate he was to play the game he loves. This mindset allowed him to pursue his passion and develop mental toughness instead of fearing failure.

Moving forward, choose to focus on the process and trust yourself more. When you direct your attention to the task rather than the "what ifs" and the "shoulds," you'll feel more confident. Replace "I should win" with "I *will execute my intentions and fight until the end.*"

I also understand that even if dropping expectations makes sense to you, it is still just an idea. Therefore, in the following chapters, I will show you *how* to turn this principle into action when it counts.

4

Trust the Process

"HEY, I'M FEELING PRETTY frustrated," Emily said, as we connected on a Zoom call.

"What's going on?" I asked.

"I just feel like I should be seeing results by now. I'm putting in the effort, but nothing seems to change," she replied, disappointed.

"I totally understand that feeling. How long have we been working together?" I asked.

"About three or four weeks," she said, pausing for a moment. "But I see other people making progress so much faster than me."

"Remember the analogy of building a house," I said. "You have to build the structure first to make sure the house is strong so it can handle the storms. This takes a little time."

Emily sighed. "But how do I know if I'm really making enough progress?"

"Think about the little victories," I replied. "You took more control over yourself in the last race, and you didn't get nearly as thrown off. You stayed in it until the end."

"That's true," she agreed. "It's hard to see this sometimes. But I guess that was a better race than the week before."

"This is all part of the process," I reminded her. "The key is how you respond in these high-pressure moments. Keep applying what you're learning. If you keep prioritizing these skills, they will be there for you. Be patient and good things will happen."

As she listened, I could see a spark of determination coming back. But clearly, more patience was going to become essential for her to stick with her goals. This is often what's missing as athletes begin to transfer the skills they're learning into actual competition.

Having patience and maintaining trust are key components in pursuing your personal goals. I know this isn't always easy to do because you may not have the evidence yet. But by focusing on small improvements, especially taking more ownership over your reactions, you can build the confidence you need to overcome almost any challenge.

Here's a powerful anecdote involving Michael Phelps, the most decorated Olympian of all time, that beautifully illustrates the idea of trusting the process in a high-stakes moment:

In the 200-meter butterfly final at the 2008 Olympics, something unexpected happened. Just moments after diving in, Phelps's goggles began to fill with water. By the halfway point of the race, he was essentially swimming blind.

But Phelps didn't panic.

Instead, he relied on the process he had rehearsed thousands of times in training. He had practiced swimming "blind" by counting strokes in case of goggle failure. He knew exactly how many strokes each lap required. He kept his rhythm, stayed composed, and trusted his muscle memory and preparation.

He finished the race, touched the wall—and won gold.

Afterward, he said:

"I couldn't see anything . . . but I had trained my body to know exactly where I was in the pool. I trusted the work."

This story is a great reminder to athletes: When chaos hits, you don't rise to the occasion—you fall back on your training. Trust the process, especially when the pressure spikes.

The path you're on now is not just about immediate results. It's also about getting better. It's about experiencing the satisfaction of using your new mastery mindset and mental skills with purpose and seeing what you can achieve.

5

Believe in Possibility

WHAT IF I COULD predict the future and told you how the rest of the season will go for you—how many events you'll win and lose, along with the scores in each one? Would you really want to know?

In fact, it's the uncertainty of the outcome that makes sports so exciting. Knowing the outcome ahead of time would actually destroy the excitement. It's the tension we feel when we don't know what will happen, combined with the motivation to win, that capture our heart, our mind, and our hopes. Without this certainty, we must confront our nerves, our thoughts, and all of the things we might imagine as possible, but can't know until they happen. Thankfully, knowing the result of an event ahead of time is impossible. However, we can wholeheartedly believe in the *possibility* of having a great day and winning, too. Believing that you *can* win is always a mindset you get to choose.

Recently, I was speaking with a new client, currently ranked top five in the world in pickleball—a sport you probably know has become incredibly popular over the past few years. Interestingly, because of his high ranking, he received a lot of sponsorship money. But shortly after this happened, his motivation dropped. This isn't uncommon. Many Olympic athletes talk about the letdown they feel *after* reaching their goals. My point is that the magic in sports is in the pursuit of the goal—with no guarantee of the outcome, maybe even not getting paid for it—while still believing in yourself anyway.

Don't get me wrong. I'm not downplaying the satisfaction of achieving a goal. I'm highlighting the opportunity to believe in yourself without needing immediate proof—or proof from your last event—that you can play well and win.

Embrace the opportunity and believe in possibility regardless of your opponent's or team's latest results. If they happen to be a level better in rankings or results, bring your focus back to your specific intentions that day. Choose to believe in yourself and your training.

However, if you've been losing more than usual lately and you're in a slump, you might wonder, *"How am I supposed to believe in myself after the last horrible game?"* I know it's tough to believe in yourself when you're struggling. Perhaps you've even been dreading games—worrying about messing up. This is yet another chance to hit the reset button and realize that every event is a new opportunity to step up and execute regardless of the past.

Let's shift your focus back into the present. Think, *"Today is a new day. I'm going all-in with my intentions. Let's see what happens."* Even if you don't feel great that day, believing in the possibility that things can turn around is a choice you get to make.

A baseball player I worked with was getting nervous about striking out before stepping into the batter's box. His nerves would be in full gear before he was even on deck. The thought kept creeping into his mind: *"You're going to strike out."* He was bracing for the worst before he even got to the plate. When he stopped trying to predict what would happen, he freed himself up. Instead of worrying about striking out, he told himself, "Maybe I will and maybe I won't." Then, he visualized making clean contact and remained in the here and now.

When you embrace the unknown, refocus on the present, and believe in possibilities, you'll feel calmer, perform at a higher level, and boost your chances of winning.

SECTION 2

Confidence & Self-Belief

WHAT IF I TOLD you that you don't need to feel confident to act confidently?

In this section, we challenge the myth that you either have confidence or you don't. True confidence is built not only from past success, but also from your ability to stay committed to yourself and your goals, regardless of the outcomes.

These chapters will help you reframe self-doubt, build an internal belief system that doesn't depend only on praise or results, and start performing from a place of trust—not tension. Whether you're coming off a slump or facing your biggest game yet, these tools will help you walk onto the field, court, track, or whatever competition you find yourself in, with your shoulders back and your mind steady.

In this section, you'll learn how to:
- Rewire the inner critic and stop overthinking.
- Perform with composure even when you're nervous.
- Build confidence through process, not perfection.

6

Act How You Want to Feel

WHEN I WAS TWELVE years old, just before my parents enrolled me in that full-time, IMG Academy in Florida (where I got disqualified for losing my cool), I was still playing baseball. It was the last game of the season, and we were in the ninth inning of my final Little League game. I knew it was my last chance to hit a home run. I hadn't hit one yet, and I really wanted to. Nothing else in the world mattered to me other than swinging at the ball with complete conviction. The score of the game was irrelevant to me at that moment. Swinging and missing, not getting on base, or striking out never occurred to me.

When it was my turn to hit, I turned to a teammate and, in a burst of confidence, declared, "Watch this. I'm going to hit it out of the park."

Walking up to the plate, I felt a sense of purpose. I told myself I was going to crush any pitch close to the plate. As the pitcher threw the first pitch, I could see it was a decent pitch—very hittable—and I locked in completely. I connected perfectly with the ball, and it soared deep toward center field. My heart raced, and I thought my dream was about to happen.

Then, unbelievably, I watched the ball hit a screw on the top of the fence and bounce back toward second base. To be honest, I was in shock. I admit that I stomped angrily on the base as my dream vanished in a split second. My hit looked like it was absolutely going to clear the fence. Instead, I ended up with a ground-rule double, which, in that moment, felt like someone punched me in the face.

Despite my momentary disappointment, I realized that when we act confidently, we can actually feel confident, too. With the clear vision in my mind of hitting a home run, I was able to create the physical presence to back it up.

Think about Steph Curry, chewing on his mouth guard. Novak Djokovic, the greatest tennis player of all time, smiling in the most pressure-filled moments. Or Michael Jordan, sticking his tongue out as he soars into the air to dunk. Why do you think these legendary athletes do these things? Because these actions help them stay loose and focused—a mental and physical state they can control. In sports, this is known as our ideal "performance state."

The best athletes use these physical cues to stay mentally and physically engaged. They also consistently repeat these cues until they become second nature.

One day, while watching a client of mine, a swimmer, I overheard her coach talking to her:

Coach: "Hey, Jordan, I noticed you hesitated a little on that dive earlier. What happened?"

Jordan: "I don't know. . . . I guess I felt a little nervous and sort of hesitated."

Coach: "I understand. But let's try to not let your feelings make the decisions. I want you to go for the dive anyway."

Jordan: "You mean, ignore what I feel?"

Coach: "Yes. In these moments, you have to trust yourself regardless. If you carry yourself with confidence, your emotions will usually follow."

Jordan: "I'll try it. Thanks, coach."

Her coach simply didn't want her emotions dictating how she approached the dive. He wanted her to trust her training anyway, to do the dive regardless of the emotions that showed up. This is all about behaving your way into a better state, not waiting to feel good. By pumping your fist after a clutch play, for example, walking as if you know exactly what you're doing, or high-fiving a teammate, you will generate more confidence.

To create your ideal performance state, stay aggressive and confident despite the errors. Do your best to commit to your intentions even though you feel nervous. Stay committed to the task at hand. I know it's really tempting to bail out when you feel pressure. This is your greatest opportunity to challenge yourself. It takes a certain commitment to yourself to act confidently when the pressure is on. If you prioritize your physical presence before you go into a game in this way, you will feel more in charge. You will think less about what might happen, or what *should* happen, because you are too busy acting how you want to be.

Going forward, when you are hesitant about taking the opportunity, do the opposite and take it. Choose to be decisive. Rather than berating yourself with thoughts like *"You suck! How could you miss that?"* you smile.

This is why Nike's slogan is so popular: "Just do it." It's hard to argue with such a powerful idea, isn't it?

With this commitment to act how you want to feel, your belief becomes unshakable. You no longer wait to feel confident.

You don't always need your thoughts to be positive to feel confident. Are you with me?

Does this sound too simple or unrealistic? I know you are used to feelings coming and going. You don't yet realize how much control you have over your state of mind by moving your body in a confident way.

Carry yourself with confidence for the next week and notice how this feels, especially after mistakes. This is not a question of whether you *can* do this. It's a matter of doing it even when you feel a little insecure.

Even when you choose to carry yourself with purpose like this, there will be times when the pressure feels too heavy and you will forget to do it. This is normal. Remember, you don't need to be perfect. But the more you do it, the more confident you will feel, and the results will follow.

7

Reframe Your Self-Doubt

IMAGINE STEPPING ONTO THE court, adrenaline pumping, anticipation buzzing in the air. You are ready to unleash your skills. You are locked in with your new mastery mindset and focused on the task at hand. But wait—suddenly, the unexpected happens. A missed shot, a fumbled pass—these moments that can break you and the team's chances of winning. Beware. This is exactly when self-doubt can bust through the open door in your mind—immediately after a mistake. If we panic, it can become a sledgehammer to our confidence. But experiencing self-doubt is also a normal reaction. However, if you can cut yourself a little slack here and stay calm, you will save yourself a ton of heartache. You will give your brain the time it needs to side-step this mental rabbit hole. This is one of the most important and challenging moments you will face in sports—another opportunity to apply your new mental skills.

As you just learned, acting confidently can make a huge difference, but you also need to accept the reality that mistakes are going to happen. I want you to expect them, but not fear them. Even the legends we admire, like Cristiano Renaldo, Steph

Curry, Aaron Judge, Michael Phelps, Roger Federer, Simone Biles, Patrick Mahomes, and others, have made more mistakes than you can count. Perfection is a myth, and even the greatest athletes stumble—often.

This is why Michael Jordan's words are so powerful: "I've failed over and over again in my life. And that is why I succeed."

Since we know that mistakes are guaranteed, letting self-doubt get the best of you—especially when you're in the middle of the competition—doesn't make a ton of sense, right? But staying calm and rational when you make a mistake is easier said than done.

I know doubt can rush in before you even know what's hit you. This is why having a tactic prepared ahead of time can help you when it takes over your brain and body.

What do mistakes mean to you? Do they mean you're not as good as you thought? That you're a choker? That you're probably going to lose? That people will think you're not as good as they thought? If you are getting consistently upset when you make a mistake, it probably means self-doubt has taken over your mind.

Don't worry. You will learn how to shut the door in your head so you can keep yourself in the game.

You see, the part of your brain that you use the most in school—called the prefrontal cortex—is not necessary in competition nearly as much as you think. The prefrontal cortex is your GPS. It breaks things down to help you get where you want to go. It helps you decide what to do next.

So, when you make a mistake and the door opens upstairs in your head, instead of letting self-doubt take over, you will be ready to reframe any negative thought that comes into your mind.

Do you want to know something most of your friends don't know? Even though a thought comes into your mind, it doesn't mean the thought is true or accurate. The cool thing is that you can start to notice when these self-doubting thoughts enter. For example, imagine you have an important game coming up and you haven't been playing well lately. Your coach is acting intensely and seems frustrated, which makes you begin to question yourself.

So, you start to imagine the worst possible scenario—playing badly, losing, or your coach getting upset. My point is that these thoughts or images in your mind don't mean that any of these things will come true. Not at all—especially when you pause and use your "school brain" for a second to change the channel or close this door. Don't be too hard on yourself if you forget. It takes time to get the hang of this.

"You have to battle with the mind just as much as you battle with the other team," says Buster Posey, All-Star and MVP for the San Francisco Giants. "Keeping a positive mindset helps in overcoming slumps."

It may be helpful for you to know that most thoughts about mistakes are rarely helpful. Instead, you can begin to coach your brain. How? By quickly "reframing" them in your head. For instance, instead of thinking, *"I messed up that play,"* you say to yourself, *"It's okay. Stay committed."* Or instead of thinking, *"What will Coach think now?"* reframe your thought to, *"He just wants to see you do what you practiced."* Ralph Waldo Emerson famously said, "For every minute you are angry, you lose sixty seconds of happiness." The translation: When self-doubt is in charge, you lose in every way.

But by reframing these unhelpful, inaccurate, and unproductive thoughts that barge through the door in your head, you will put yourself in the driver's seat—in control, with the updated GPS guiding you toward the best performances of your life.

8

Give Yourself Permission to Miss

IMAGINE HAVING THE PERMISSION to make mistakes—to miss the layup, the sitter overhead, the three-foot putt, or a slow start to the race. In other words, since you rationally know that the best athletes make errors all the time, you decide ahead of time that you're going to accept and not overreact to mistakes before your competition. You decide that you will simply move on instantly.

This is not a free pass to accept errors because you're not as good as you think. This is not what I mean at all. In fact, I'm arguing that you are better than you think and that making mistakes doesn't change this in the slightest. What I want you to see is how much better you can play when you give yourself more freedom to miss. Ironically, when you add this principle to your toolkit, you will begin to make fewer mistakes over time.

Giving yourself what I call a "permission slip," you will be more willing to take calculated risks under pressure. You will also find that you are more decisive, both of which will help you improve faster and become an even better athlete.

A twelve-year-old football player, who is quite small for his age (let's call him Hudson) shared a memorable moment with me during one of our sessions when I asked about one of his best games: In the last few minutes of the final game—the Super Bowl—his team is down by one touchdown. When the quarterback tosses Hudson the ball, he spots an opening and surges forward—five yards, then ten. Suddenly, he sees a kid barreling toward him with his head down. Hudson faces a choice: go around him, be defensive and take the hit, or aggressively charge straight at him. In that split second, Hudson gives himself permission to go straight at the kid, even if it doesn't end up being the right decision. Helmets clash loudly, and to his surprise, the other kid goes down.

But it's not over. Out of nowhere, an even bigger player comes straight at Hudson, also with his head down, clearly ready to take him out. He hears the crowd, including his parents and their friends, cheering loudly from the sidelines. With this bigger kid coming straight at him, Hudson, again, decides to not back down and goes directly at him. Astonishingly, the big kid goes down, too. Hudson breaks free and scores a touchdown in the final seconds of the game. As a funny aside, little Hudson gets a new nickname, Mad Dog.

By choosing to be aggressive, Hudson's decision paid off. Although it seemed risky at first, with the outcome far from guaranteed, it was his willingness to embrace that risk—the permission he gave himself in that moment—that created the opportunity for such a successful play.

Knowing how much smaller he was than almost every other kid on the field, Hudson's choice wasn't easy. It took courage to be willing to get knocked to the ground and risk the embarrassment, not to mention injury. When we try to not look bad and remain defensive, we usually make worse decisions and more mistakes. Giving yourself permission to miss will help you compete with more freedom. By accepting and *applying* this principle, you will bounce back faster and win more.

Remember Michael Jordan's powerful admission: "I've missed more than nine thousand shots in my career. I've lost almost three hundred games. Twenty-six times, I've been trusted to take the game-winning shot, and I missed. I've failed over and over again in my life. And that is why I succeed." Jordan believed that learning from setbacks and remaining dedicated to long-term goals, despite facing disappointment and defeat, is the key to success.

His willingness to take the shot and fall short is an example of this "permission slip" that he would give to himself. It's easiest to take risks and go for the goal when you're feeling confident and playing well, but will you allow yourself the same freedom after you miss a penalty kick or overthrow a pass? In these moments, a big part of you might think it is reckless, even stupid, to give yourself this freedom—especially after just making a mistake. Is this really the best approach after a mistake? It's a fair question.

It's actually more important to give yourself this added freedom in these moments. In fact, this is exactly when you can make the most progress in your sport. Sure, you might need to refocus on one intention to get your stride back (i.e., be present, stay positive, trust your body, be patient). But it is very likely that your performance is suffering because you aren't giving yourself this permission—this freedom—from the start of the event.

Again, giving yourself permission to miss is not to be confused with being passive and not caring. On the contrary, this principle encourages you to stay mentally strong and more committed in tough situations. You understand there is always an opportunity to improve, even in the final minutes of a game. You always believe that there is a chance to turn things around even when it looks bleak.

This mental shift may seem hard at first because it asks you to choose courage over safety. But as an athlete, this risk will be worth the investment. Trust me.

There is one more reward you'll get when you give yourself permission to miss. You will learn skills faster and make better adjustments because you aren't letting frustration take over.

At first, this "permission slip" may sound like it conflicts with messages you are getting about the importance of not missing or the goal of trying to be more consistent. But it isn't. You can do both at the same time. Ultimately, this is about using your new mastery mindset as a weapon. By giving yourself more "permission slips," you will have a big edge over your competitors.

9

Develop Unconditional Confidence

MOST ATHLETES KNOW THAT winning is the quickest way to boost their confidence. But what happens when you have off days and lose a few times in a row? Without the wins, many athletes, even coaches, find their confidence dropping just as fast.

This is why I want you to develop something I call "unconditional confidence." What this means is that even when you don't achieve your own performance goals or win on any given day, you don't allow your confidence to disappear. Unconditional confidence is a deeper belief in your skills, your athleticism, your ability to adapt and learn, and a commitment to the things you have control over—namely, *you*.

The drop in confidence happens automatically, doesn't it? In Chapter 7, "Reframe Your Self-Doubt," we explored how quickly self-doubt can come knocking on your door. But unconditional confidence is like having an impenetrable shield in your mind. A bad day, or even a loss, just bounces off. It might take a few hours, but you reset, reflect, and reengage in the pursuit of mastery. You know that whatever happened will only make you better in the long run.

As I indicated above, to cultivate more unconditional confidence, you need to broaden your definition of confidence to include your positive qualities, including your motivation to improve your mental game. But I understand winning and losing have been your main, perhaps only, metrics until now. This is your challenge and opportunity now—to expand your perspective about what makes you great.

I trust you agree that having more ways to fuel your confidence would be helpful. The key is to remember that you have a choice about how you think about yourself, especially when you are feeling tense or emotional. Applying the concept of unconditional confidence is where the rubber meets the road. Talk is cheap. Eventually, you have to know you're better than you think and act like you are.

Simone Biles, one of the best Olympic gymnasts of all time, said, "Confidence is not thinking you'll never lose; it's knowing you'll be okay no matter what happens."

Again, believe it or not, it's the small improvements, the adjustments you make, the attitude you choose, the willingness to go for it when you're nervous—these are the new metrics that will give you a huge boost of lasting confidence.

Think about it. If you depend only on winning or validation from other people to feel confident, you give away your power. You are no longer in control. This leads to more self-doubt and fear of failure. But emphasizing the "controllables" will protect you from big dips in confidence, so your wins can carry you even further down the field.

Confidence is about who you are, not something you earn only when things go well. Even in games when the late and great

Kobe Bryant missed, he never stopped believing that he was the best one to take the next shot. "I'd rather go 0-for-30 than 0–9," Kobe said. "Because that means you stopped shooting. That means you lost confidence."

Confidence isn't earned when things go well—it's revealed when things get hard. That's unconditional confidence.

10

Beware of the Mind-Reading Trap

Imagine you're sitting down on the bleachers in the gym or on the stairs at practice, and your coach says, "I'd like you to close your eyes for two minutes because there's a secret you're about to discover."

Then he adds, "There is something that each of you does all the time. We all do it without even realizing it. After about a minute, he gives another hint to the team, "You're probably doing it right now, too."

Before the two minutes are up, one of your teammates begins to chuckle to herself. Then another. Gradually, one by one, most of your teammates are either quietly laughing or smiling about something. You're pretty sure you know what it is, too, but you're not 100 percent sure.

"Seems like a few of you might be aware of this little secret," the coach says, also with a slight smile, as he sees you and the rest of the team beginning to pick up on it. "Does anyone want to share what they noticed?" he continues.

"Well," says one of your teammates, "when you said, 'You're probably doing it right now,' I figured it had something to do with how awkward I felt because I was thinking other people might be judging me. I just got self-conscious for some reason."

"Exactly!" acknowledged the coach. "How many of you thought the same thing?" he asked. More than half of the team's hands went up.

"How many of you do this in your own life?" he inquires again. All the hands go up this time. "Yes, this is the secret," he acknowledges to the team. "We worry about what other people think about us. We barely even notice it because we do it all the time. It's kind of interesting, isn't it?"

I'm sharing this scene to help you see that this is something many athletes struggle with—and you're not alone. You likely do this more than you realize, especially after mistakes. Maybe you think to yourself, *"How embarrassing. What will people say if we lose?"* Once you become aware of this trap—trying to read other people's minds—you can notice these thoughts and either reframe them or change the channel. It can help when you realize that instead of worrying about you, other people are usually thinking about themselves.

When we worry about what other people think about us, once again, we are giving our power away.

It's natural to want other people to respect us. We want to feel like we belong. It's true that the more people like us, the more opportunities will come our way. The problem isn't that we care about what other people think; it's that we allow this built-in need to go too far. We know it's gone too far when other people's opinions begin to matter more than our own.

In sports—and in life—this high need for approval will eventually steer you into some dark waters. At some point, you will find yourself unhappy and underperforming but not know why. When you spend too much time seeking praise from others and worrying about what they think about you, you will avoid opportunities and shrink under pressure. But you might need to hit this wall to realize what you're doing isn't really working anymore.

Performing at your highest level happens when you are more internally motivated—playing for yourself or your team, rather than always trying to satisfy other people. I recognize that at your age, this may seem like a stretch because your coach and parents are so involved. But this doesn't mean you can't ask yourself what you think, what you want to do, and whether you agree with the feedback you're hearing. For now, it's helpful to just be aware of this concept of intrinsic (for you) vs. extrinsic motivation (other people and trophies). It's normal to have both.

For a moment, let's return to the earlier scene when your teammates became aware of this mind-reading trap—the tendency to worry about what other people are thinking about you.

Let's test this out: Think about one of your good friend's recent wins, an error by a teammate, or imagine your favorite athlete who had a bad day recently.

How long did you think about your friend, teammate, or favorite athlete when they fell short? Do you think less of this person now? When I ask this question, most athletes say they dwell on a mistake for ten seconds to a minute—maybe a few hours when their favorite team or an athlete they love suffers a close loss. I imagine it's similar for you. So why assume others are thinking about your mistake a hundred times longer than you think about theirs? Interesting, isn't it? Then, consider how much time we spend worrying about something that isn't actually happening!

If you care about your sport—as I'm sure you do—you are going to get upset when you don't play well and lose. It stings. You think about all the things you could have done differently. This is bad enough. But it gets worse. Then, you imagine other people's reactions. You're convinced they will think less of you, maybe even ignore you.

But remember, these real or imaginary people (other than your coach and parents) are not thinking about you beyond the actual event. We just proved that, didn't we? When the event is over, people return to their lives and their own worries. It's a fact.

"We cannot live being obsessed with what other people think about us," warns Cristiano Ronaldo, five-time FIFA player of the year. "It's impossible to live like that. Not even God managed to please the entire world."

I remember running into a coach at Stanford I knew well. He looked deep in thought. So, I asked him what was going on.

He looked up and, knowing what I do for a living, said, "I've just been thinking a lot about my players' biggest struggle. They are so distracted and tight lately. They are totally caught up worrying about what I, their teammates, and even their friends think about them. It's just getting worse."

"Are they aware they're doing this?" I ask.

He looked surprised by my question. "I don't know for sure," he acknowledged. "I don't think so."

"I think this would be a good place to start," I replied. "Once they are aware of this trap, they can begin to do something about it. Right now, it's a mental habit they aren't even aware they have."

"True," the coach acknowledged. "I'll definitely bring this up in our next team meeting."

Worrying about others' opinions is something we all do—it shows that you want to be respected and feel successful, which is great. You're driven. Now it's about finding balance and building your own internal system of validation, so you don't rely as much on outside approval.

This is a battle worth fighting. When you start worrying about others' opinions, remind yourself of your skills, your progress, and your ability to succeed on your own terms.

SECTION 3

Focus & Attention Control

WHEN THE PRESSURE HITS, can you stay locked in?

In this section, you'll develop the mental skill of focus—what to pay attention to, when to reset it, and how to keep your mind from drifting to distractions or doubts.

Whether it's your phone, the crowd, or your own thoughts pulling you away from the moment, focus can be trained like a muscle. These chapters show you how to manage that focus in both training and competition so that you're fully present when it counts most.

In this section, you'll learn how to:
- Train your brain to stay in the moment
- Use journaling and visualization to sharpen awareness
- Limit distractions and protect your mental space

11

Prioritize Your Focus

YOU MAY HAVE HEARD of the legendary Michael Jordan and his iconic "flu game" during the 1997 NBA Finals. Despite being severely ill—even vomiting during the game—he led the Chicago Bulls to victory against the Utah Jazz, scoring thirty-eight points to clinch the NBA title. Hall of Fame coach Jerry Sloan remarked on Jordan's remarkable performance, saying, "He played extremely well, and I had no idea he was even sick."

Jordan's performance while battling the flu shows the determination and focus shared by all elite athletes. This is your challenge as well: to engage fully in the task at hand and on what you control, regardless of the circumstances.

But being this focused when you're not feeling well isn't easy. Think about how long you can keep your attention before it begins to wander. You probably text, scroll through Instagram, watch TikTok, or view YouTube videos while you're doing homework. The fact is, we are teaching ourselves to be unfocused as we constantly switch between snaps, apps, and videos. Deep focus is becoming much harder to achieve, and this is very relevant to you as an athlete.

Now, let's dive into the different types of focus available to you so you can begin to build this muscle. First, I want you to understand that we cannot focus on two things at once. This is important because it puts the remote control in your hand.

For example, imagine you have the ball and you're about to score a goal in soccer. You quickly notice where the goalie is and identify the part of the net you want to aim for. Even though it might feel like you're focused on both at the same time, you're switching attention between them in a split second. What you did was register the goalie's position—then you chose your target. It all happens fast, but in that critical moment when it's time to shoot, you must choose—do I focus on the pressure around me, or do I lock in on the ball and the shot?

This matters for a lot of reasons, which we'll explore next.

What is helpful to understand is that, in any given moment, we have the choice to focus our attention internally (thoughts, tactics, visuals) or we can place our focus externally (goalie, ball, teammate, net). In the example above, if you had a last-second thought—*"Don't miss!"*—this would be an internal focus. As you probably already know, when you are in your head thinking—especially in these crucial moments—the outcome is usually not positive.

Do you see the difference? Focus includes both dimensions—internal and external. Both are necessary, and choosing the right "channel" will depend on the situation. But focusing mostly externally will be best.

In my coaching practice, sometimes I meet athletes where they practice—soccer field, golf course, basketball court, tennis court, or even in the batting cage—to observe their focus firsthand. One day, I was pitching to a baseball player in a cage (I was a pitcher as a kid, so I can sometimes reach back and find a little magic), and he was crushing my pitches. Then, out of nowhere, he started whiffing. It was so abrupt, I paused and asked him, "Where did your focus go?"

In a daze, he replied slowly, "Uh, I'm not really sure."

"Really? You're not sure?" I asked.

Sometimes athletes will say they don't know, but that's just their first knee-jerk answer. It can be useful to pause and take your time to think about these types of questions, especially if you've never thought about it before.

With a few more seconds to ponder my question, he finally acknowledged, "Actually, I was thinking about a few different things—the test I have tomorrow and my game this weekend."

"Does losing focus like this happen often?" I asked.

"All the time," he replied.

It turned out that this athlete found himself inside his head (internally focused) most of the time. Until I asked him, he hadn't been aware of it. I wasn't surprised. Most young athletes don't yet realize there are different levels of focus.

Of course, when we are in our heads thinking about the future, we can't focus on the task at hand in the present. Internal distractions happen all the time in practice, and this is a perfect opportunity to refocus on something specific in the moment— like the ball, for instance.

Practice also won't feel as important as competition, so your adrenaline—and focus—may be lower. That makes it the perfect time to train your focus for game day.

Distractions are also constant when you compete: the coach shouting instructions from the sidelines, threatening to pull you out; teammates criticizing you; the pressure of the score when it's close; parents in the stands holding their breath; and the looming worry about what your friends will say if you lose. Therefore, you need to prioritize and guard your focus.

It is up to you to change the channel and return to the present. Nobody can do this for you. Therefore, we need to keep building the remote control together.

When you realize you are in your head, it's best to refocus to something externally (i.e., changing the channel from your coach's angry face [external] to a quick image of the ball swooshing into the basket [internal]).

Your mind can shift between the past, present, and future—but only focus on one at a time. The same goes for internal and external focus. Staying present is always the goal.

As you become more aware of your focusing tendencies, you will be able to refocus on what's relevant in the moment. Being present means not worrying about your homework during practice (future). It means you are not replaying an earlier, awkward conversation before your event (past) or worrying about the outcome (future). When you're fully present, this mental clutter fades away, and you choose to engage in the here and now.

Isn't it annoying how you can be totally locked in before a game and then suddenly have your mind take off on you? Awareness will help. Just this week, a closing pitcher told me, "Just when I was about to close out the inning, I had a thought: Don't choke this. But right when I realized it, I slapped my leg and it switched my focus. It worked. I closed it out."

From time to time, ask yourself if you are in the past, present, or future.

Imagine training your mind like you would train a new puppy dog. You need to watch the dog because if you don't keep an eye on it, it might leave a mess (like cluttered thoughts) all over your mental headspace.

"The only way I was able to pick up details on the court, to be aware of the minutiae on the hardwood, was by training my mind to do that off the court and focusing on every detail in my daily life," said Kobe Bryant.

I discovered the same technique when I was playing the pro tennis tour. Before an event, I purposely tracked things with my eyes for a few seconds longer off the court—like license plates when riding in the car and menus when ordering food. Additionally, focusing on my breath helped me narrow my focus before the match started. These techniques can bring you into the present and make you feel more in control of the one thing you do control—yourself, and where you put your attention in any moment.

Here's my invitation to you: Before your event, set an intention to be present and to refocus your mind when it wanders, both on and off the field. Do it in your classes, too, especially if you have a boring class. It is almost a guarantee that your mind will wander there. It will also wander during practice and when you're doing homework at night. Start to notice when your mind drifts to the future and the past. Becoming aware of this tendency to wander is a great start. It's not easy, but you can build on this once you start paying attention more often. I promise it will pay off in big ways for you.

Avoid rushing, be intentional about staying calm, and try not to let your eyes dart around too much. We lose focus when we're anxious or trying to do too much too fast.

I think you'll be surprised how prioritizing your focus—especially when you focus externally—will lift performance. Shifting your attention with this imaginary remote control will help you spend more time in the present and out of your head so you can perform at your highest level more often.

12

Play on Your Own Terms

"WHEN I'M OLDER, IF I have my own apartment, a microwave, and TV, I'll be happy," admitted one of my clients, a junior in high school at the time.

Josh initially came to see me because he was lonely and felt badly about himself. This is a true story and one of the most gratifying experiences of my career.

This boy didn't have many friends, and I could tell he wasn't ready for any strategies or tools yet. He needed connection. He had no self-confidence, and the idea of "playing on his terms"—choosing his own path—was a million miles away in his mind.

So, every Wednesday, we would meet at a local restaurant and have soup together. I don't know why he chose soup—maybe because it soothed him—but once we ordered it the first time, it became our routine.

Josh was remarkably open with me, telling me about his tendency to blurt things out at the wrong time because of his ADHD, that he had no real friends to speak of, and his lack of motivation for the future.

Eventually, I tried to point out how he was falling into some of the mental traps you learned in Chapter 10, "Beware of the Mind-Reading Trap," and a few others—namely, the all-or-nothing trap—where we think things are either great or horrible. But I hit a brick wall. He understood the idea, but he didn't have the confidence that he could do anything with it. I wasn't surprised by this, but I felt I had to try.

We met for over a year and a half, and to be honest, I didn't think I helped him at all. He graduated from high school and then attended college. I didn't hear from him until I received this email ten years later.

> Jeff, it's been quite a while. Lately, I've been thinking back to my high school years and remember telling you that if I could live in a one-bedroom apartment with a microwave and TV, I'd be happy. That seems incredible to me now. I thought you should know that since graduating high school, I graduated as the valedictorian in college, moved to Japan to study international business, got a black belt in karate, and I'm engaged to be married.
>
> I wanted you to know that if you ever doubt that you are helping people, just think of me, because I couldn't have done this without you. If you can save one life, it's worth it, and you saved mine.

Of course, tears were streaming down my face as I read his email. But I have to tell you the follow-up to this because it truly made me realize that anything is possible when you decide to take ownership over your life, to play on your terms.

A few years later, I'm in the checkout line at the local grocery store and Josh spots me.

"Jeff, it's Josh. How are you?" he says excitedly.

"Oh my God, Josh," I say. "You have to be kidding." I am dying to know what he's up to.

"Do you have a couple of minutes to catch up?" he asks.

"Absolutely," I say with excitement.

Well, get this—when I ask Josh what he's up to now, he says, "I can't really tell you. It's top secret. Let's just say it has something to do with the FBI."

You can see why I was blown away by this experience. Even though Josh was not a high-level athlete, his story is a powerful example of the strength we all have when we play on our own terms and decide that other people, society, external circumstances, or our personal weaknesses will not keep us down. Playing on our own terms means that we put ourselves in the driver's seat of our lives and make choices that reflect our highest vision of ourselves. This takes courage. But when we begin to see our strengths more clearly and filter out the noise, our dreams have room to trickle in. Then, when we're ready, we can choose to go for it—on our terms.

Whether it's on the field or off, you are going to have some days when you just can't find your magic. You'll wonder why you didn't catch your mistakes during the competition. It will feel like a blur. But if you remain curious and pay attention, you will notice thoughts such as, *"I can't do it. I'm never going to get it right."*

Sometimes it's clear what happened. Other times, it's not. But if you take responsibility for yourself, you will see that your mistakes are usually caused by something you had control over—something you can also learn from and improve.

One thing is always certain—the fix will be within you. It is about taking charge of yourself—your thoughts, mood, and behavior—and making your own decisions.

I imagine you have been in many tough situations already—whether it's deciding to shoot when the game is on the line, dealing with negative comments from a teammate, choosing between high school sports and a travel team, balancing two different sports and getting your schoolwork done, and deciding which AP classes you should take or where you want to go to college, among others.

Having to deal with this pressure now will help you make healthier decisions in the future. In fact, it is these challenges you wish would go away that are the building blocks to creating the best version of yourself.

This is why I am highlighting the concept of "playing on your terms" in this chapter, because it will help you excel in these difficult situations with the following principles:

- I act confidently even if I don't feel it.
- I play aggressively when the game is on the line.
- I let mistakes go quickly.
- I embrace pressure.
- I trust my instincts and assert myself with my teammates and with my coach when I'm upset.

Playing on your terms means that you don't accept poor behavior from others out of fear—fear of their reaction, fear of losing playing time, or fear of feeling anxious. You begin to take responsibility, rather than doing nothing. You think about what's best for you in the long run, not just the moment.

You cannot force or predict an outcome. But, like Josh, you too can choose your thoughts, your actions, and even your feelings, and make magic happen. Once you put yourself in the driver's seat of your life, there is no stopping you. Find your music, play it, and don't stop playing it.

13

Journal for Optimal Performance

ANNA HALL, A TRACK and field star competing in seven events, faced a daunting setback. Five months before the Olympic Trials, she injured her knee and needed surgery. With the countdown timer ticking, the possibility of competing was dwindling fast.

Anna was feeling a lot of anxiety and self-doubt. Instinctively, she started writing about her thoughts and feelings. She said, "Mentally, I think the US Olympic Trials is the most challenging event that we'll do . . . it doesn't matter if I wake up sick, or if I wake up and my knee is swollen. You just have to find a way to make it happen."

Hall used journaling to keep her focused, motivated, and in a positive frame of mind when she was feeling down: "The night before competition, I'll write down things that I want to feel tomorrow," Hall acknowledged. "I don't always even believe it when I'm writing it. But I'm telling myself tomorrow, when I wake up, this is who I am. So that's something that has helped me a lot."

Her coach also recognized that journaling played a vital role in her success, providing her with the mental clarity needed not only to compete but also to win the gold medal. "Today," she penned, "I will become an Olympian." And she did.

Anna's story is just one of many illustrating how writing serves as a powerful tool for top athletes. There are so many challenges you face every week. You are driven. You want to play well and win. You want to do well in school. It seems like everyone is doing well, and you may feel like it's hard to keep up. What usually gets lost in this day-to-day juggle is awareness and perspective, which are key not only for our health and happiness but also for making important adjustments along the way.

Writing about your feelings, like Anna Hall started to do prior to the Olympics, can help you reset. Science backs this up. It will lower your stress and help you feel more optimistic about the future.

I recall a seventeen-year-old high school athlete walking into my office, feeling like her life was spiraling out of control. "My mind races," she admitted. "I worry all the time, and I can't sleep."

However, halfway through our meeting, she seemed calmer. "Do you notice a difference in how you feel right now, since we started talking today?" I asked.

"Yeah, I guess I do," she replied. "I'm not as stressed out."

"Exactly," I affirmed. "That's because you're talking through your feelings. It helps clear the mind when we reflect on what's happening inside of us."

I also let her know she could do this for herself through consistent journaling. She bought a notebook that week and started writing down her thoughts every night for a few minutes before bed. Given how much time she was spending on screens outside of homework, I knew this was going to be a stretch for her.

Then one day she decided to give it a try. She started writing about the things she wanted to improve and the intentions she wanted to prioritize in each practice. She would do the same before games. She also wrote about some of her relationships outside of sports. Here are some of the things that came out of her journaling:

- Think before you act instead of stressing about it afterwards.
- Just go for it and stop worrying about what others think.
- You're better than you think.
- If you keep working on your cardio and trust yourself, good things will happen.

By the time she finished writing, she would always find something positive about her situation. Even when she felt a bit down about her life and performance, writing always seemed to make her feel better. Putting her thoughts down on paper helped her think things through instead of letting them get stuck in her head. She became more aware of her reactions under pressure and turned her problems into solvable challenges. Instead of viewing herself as a failure, she became more accepting of mistakes. Usually, her performance and mood improved within days, if not the very next day.

If you decide to write—or record your thoughts on your phone—it's very important to be completely honest with yourself, even if it feels uncomfortable. Being aware of your feelings and observing your thoughts takes courage and patience. When you do this, you will notice that your mind will start to calm down as you go inward. If you decide to journal after your events, your observations will be most fresh within twenty minutes afterward. But journaling the same night or even the next day is still beneficial. This journal is for you, nobody else.

It's easy to avoid reflecting because it requires extra mental effort. You may also feel that it's not worth the time because it's not as concrete as practicing your specific skills in your sport. You will also be pulled back to your phone because it offers quick and easy entertainment.

However, going inside and reflecting on things will pay you back many times over. Anna Hall and many other Olympic athletes understand the power of the written word to help them become peak performers. This powerful tool is also available to you when you are ready.

14

Visualize Before and During Competition

CONSIDER THE LEGENDARY LATE basketball player Kobe Bryant, who had an insatiable desire to win. Even from a young age, he was known for his extraordinary work ethic and dedication to basketball. A crucial part of his preparation involved seeing himself play in his mind before he even went onto the basketball court.

I bet you have also imagined yourself performing in your sport without even realizing it. It's a natural process as your brain prepares you for competition.

Kobe often spoke about his pre-game routine, where he would go through plays in his mind to boost his confidence and narrow his focus. He would sit quietly, clear his mind, and pull up images of himself performing well, scoring amazing shots, and leading his team to victory. These mental images empowered him, creating a sense of confidence and clarity.

One day, prior to the crucial Game 7 of the NBA Finals, Kobe engaged in an intense session of visualization. He recalled moments from past games where he succeeded under pressure, coupled with a vivid picture of how the game would feel. When game time arrived, he felt like a lion unleashed, prepared for battle. For Kobe, visualization was not merely a technique; it was a fundamental factor in his success as an athlete.

Nearly all Olympic athletes have reported utilizing visualization as a preparation tool for competition.

To practice visualization, start by calming your mind and body with deep abdominal breaths for a couple of minutes (you will learn this technique in Chapter 19, "Breathe with Intention"). Find a quiet space where you can focus on your breathing. Once you feel calm, imagine executing your favorite moves. Visualize yourself as an active participant, feeling the energy of each moment as you perform. If immersing yourself feels challenging, you can also visualize it from an external perspective, like watching yourself on a highlight reel. The key is to feel yourself executing each move and connecting the images with excitement and enthusiasm. If you can see and feel it in your mind, you can do it when it counts, too.

It can help to follow these five guidelines:

1. Take a few minutes to write down the qualities of your best performance (calm, aggressive, having fun, high intensity, etc.).

2. Use deep breathing to calm your mind for a few minutes.

3. Gradually picture specific moments in competition using the qualities you wrote down that you want to emphasize.

4. Enjoy this exercise and don't worry if you make a few mistakes while visualizing. Stick with it and see yourself smiling, shrugging these off, and adjusting.

5. Do this in the car on the way to the event, while waiting to start the race, or before you are called into the game. Even just a few minutes can increase your confidence.

Visualization can also help you speed up your learning and skill development. By creating certain moves or introducing new tactics in your mind, you will strengthen the nerves in your brain—something called the myelin sheath—and begin to trust yourself more under pressure.

There is another hidden advantage when you take time to visualize. Choosing to do it takes initiative. It requires motivation. Instead of being passive and hoping you have a good day, you prepare with purpose. By visualizing yourself performing ahead of time, you are reinforcing the belief that you are in control of yourself. You recognize that your mind-body state will be determined by you and not the external environment. Picturing your best moves and feeling it in your mind will only increase the odds that you do it again. Seeing is believing.

15

Put Your Phone Away Before the Game

I KNOW IT CAN sometimes be difficult to put our phones away, even if the starting time is getting close. We have a little extra time on our hands, and we don't feel like getting into some big conversation immediately before we play anyway. In these moments, it may be tempting to reach for your phone and scroll. But if you resist the urge, redirect your focus to the present moment and breathe, you will end up performing a lot better. Which dimension of focus do you want to be in? Remember, not the past or future, but the present. If you can set boundaries around your phone time on game day, it will help you get closer to your ideal performance state—the ultimate experience for any athlete.

Consider what three-time Grand Slam champion Andy Murray did to help him manage his phone and social media habit: "I don't have Twitter on my phone, and I deleted Instagram last week. I'm done. I deleted it all off my phone," he said.

Research shows that spending time on social media can hurt performance. In a study of over four thousand tennis matches, it was found that players' moods, which were reflected in their social media activity, directly impacted the quality of their performance.

So, why does using your phone before you compete have this kind of impact? This is due to something called "distraction-conflict theory." When you're scrolling through your phone, your brain gets pulled away from the moment. This distraction can change your mood and make it harder to shift back to the narrower focus you need for competition. Too much information from social media can also overwhelm you and make it harder to make good decisions.

It's understandable that you will feel nervous before competing and may want to distract yourself. You might even feel anxious when you're not connected to your phone. This has become more common.

Interestingly, Kliff Kingsbury, head coach of the Arizona Cardinals in the NFL, has introduced "cell phone breaks" during team meetings to help players who struggle with their focus. "When you start to see their hands twitching and legs shaking, you know they need that social media fix," Kingsbury says. "So, we let them hop on for a bit before getting back to the meeting to refocus." It's all about finding a balance and using technology in a healthy way if you want to perform at your highest level more consistently.

Think about how you feel after spending time on your phone. Do you notice a change in your focus and energy? It can really split your concentration. When you finally put your phone down, it takes extra energy to switch back to what you were doing. Plus, if you happen to see a negative message right before a game, that can pull your attention away even more.

Many athletes find social media frustrating because it also feels superficial. One athlete shared, "It just sucks that people think social media reflects your day exactly when it doesn't. I could run for eight hours and then post a selfie at dinner, and people would think that's all I did. It's exhausting."

Tennis star Coco Gauff is known for taking breaks from her phone and limiting her social media time. "I wish I would have known earlier not to focus on social media so much," she admits.

NBA superstar Stephen Curry recently discussed the pressures of social media in an interview with CNN, saying, "This is a new era regarding the spotlight on every NBA athlete and athletes in general. The expectations are on us every single day."

Next time you feel the urge to reach for your phone, remember there may be a consequence you don't like. It is worth reminding yourself that you can check it right after the event. Think about all the effort you've put into preparing for this game. Wouldn't it be a shame to destroy your chances of executing because you allowed yourself to be pulled into an entirely different dimension?

I strongly encourage you to trust the research and adopt the pre-game routines of the most successful athletes. Challenge yourself: Put your phone away, close your eyes, visualize yourself executing your intentions, and let your mind settle into a focused, distraction-free zone that's just for you.

SECTION 4

Self-Regulation & Recovery

YOU CAN'T ALWAYS CONTROL what happens—but you can control how you respond.

This section is about learning to regulate your body and emotions under pressure. That means staying calm when things speed up, finding stillness before a big moment, and knowing how to reset when frustration builds.

These tools aren't just for tough games—they're essential for recovery, practice quality, and long-term performance health. If you want to avoid burnout and stay mentally sharp, this is where it starts.

In this section, you'll learn how to:

- Manage nerves, stress, and anxiety in the moment.
- Use breath, body, and rhythm to reset your system.
- Recover faster—mentally and emotionally.

16

Create a New Relationship with Your Nerves

BUCKLE UP. YOU DON'T want to miss out on what's coming next. Think about this chapter as the play button on the inner remote control we are building together—the same button you use to play video games or watch Netflix.

Every athlete knows the experience of "choking" under pressure. Devastating losses and unexplained drops in performance are part of every athlete's experience on the path toward mastery. Call it what you want—nerves, adrenaline, tightness, or fear. It's also called performance anxiety. You know the feeling— your mind starts racing with doubts about the upcoming event. You feel as though a hundred butterflies just dropped into your stomach. Maybe you even feel a little sick and have the urge to throw up. I have seen all kinds of reactions to this surge of adrenaline. You might be thinking, *"Oh, no. I'm tight. Not again. I hate this feeling."* If this is the case, you have nothing to feel ashamed about. This is just another challenge to master, and it will become a game-changer when you do.

Performance anxiety happens because we think we might lose. It comes on when we worry about disappointing our parents and coaches. Sometimes it feels like it comes out of nowhere, doesn't it? Even if we're feeling pretty good about our latest practices, stress about things off the field can show up and make us feel tense.

You're not alone if you find yourself wishing this anxiety would just go away. I don't want to disappoint you, but it's not going anywhere until you change your reaction to it. What do I mean? When you feel nerves, adrenaline, or tightness, and think: "I can't wait to play. This is going to be exciting," you will put yourself on the path toward freedom.

In other words, you need to accept and embrace this adrenaline when it spikes. This is what makes competition so challenging and exhilarating! But this means you need to be unfazed by negative thoughts or when that butterfly feeling shows up in your stomach. You have some adrenaline flowing through your body? Awesome.

Novak Djokovic, the greatest tennis player of all time, recently said, "I think all this positive thinking stuff is ridiculous. Of course you are going to have negative thoughts. I have them all the time. I just don't stay there as long as I used to, and I can reset pretty quickly now."

Managing your negative thoughts will help you to get to know your brain a little better, so you can start coaching it— that's right, you coach it. You will learn how to use your new remote control to choose which thoughts you want to keep and which you want to let go of.

Did you know that worrying about the future is a skill we developed thousands of years ago? Anticipating the future helped humans avoid predators who were trying to kill them. This advanced skill is the reason you are alive and reading this book right now. But I want you to understand that your brain doesn't know the difference between that make-or-break moment in the game and the possibility of being eaten for dinner. Think about this. It's biologically true. This is why the nerves feel so intense sometimes. Your brain can behave as if winning or losing feels like life or death. When you go into fear mode and feel tight and anxious, it's because your brain is doing what it was designed to do. That's why we need to develop a new reaction when all this stuff happens on the inside.

The point is you can choose a different thought and a different reaction when you feel nervous. You can begin to accept and ignore the worries about the outcome. The nerves don't mean that something bad is going to happen. They don't mean that you've lost your confidence.

Even though losing can really hurt, by now you also understand that it's not as bad as your brain is making it seem. Within a day or two, you're back at practice and working on your skills. Yes, the fear might linger for a few days—I get it. But it passes. I encourage you not to believe everything you think. Even though you feel tight or nervous, it doesn't mean you have to perform this way. Remember, you're playing the sport you love. Even if you lose, you will learn from it, the pain will pass, and people will forget.

You are responsible for your reactions. You must push the reset button.

I know the surge of adrenaline can feel uncomfortable. But it's also important to know that it will gradually fade when you start accepting that it is normal, even if it doesn't seem that way in the moment. Nerves come and go because you care about what you're doing. It's up to you to make sure you use this energy in a positive way. Would you rather be lying on your couch at home watching TV or pushing yourself to the limit in the pursuit of another win?

A few years ago, I worked with a successful but anxious world-class skier. He was scared about repeating a bad performance on the course he had struggled with a year before. So, we worked together to build the same mastery mindset you're learning now. As the Olympic Trials were coming up, his anxiety started to get the best of him. Understandably, he was worried about feeling the same adrenaline again.

As you are beginning to learn, wanting to avoid nerves only makes it worse. Believe it or not, we can even get nervous about being nervous, which is natural but no longer necessary. How do the best athletes use these feelings to play better? Instead of worrying about the butterflies in their stomach, they change the channel on their inner remote control and focus on the hoop, the goal, the service box, their shot, or the weaknesses of their opponent—remember that *external* focus? They shift their focus from themselves to the task in front of them.

The adrenaline they feel becomes their mental edge under pressure. What these athletes understand—and what you will soon see for yourself—is that managing and using this adrenaline is the main goal of competition. Mentally tough athletes want to see how well they can perform regardless of the situation, with or without nerves. Tiger Woods said, "If you don't feel nervous, that means you don't care about how you play. I care about how I play."

Think about your own reaction when you feel your heart starting to beat faster. Do you panic and think, *"Oh, no. You'd better play it safe?"*

Let's go one layer deeper. Why do we automatically think nerves are negative, anyway? Do you know that the feelings of excitement and fear are close cousins? In other words, they are very similar in how they affect our bodies. So, why don't we naturally see adrenaline as an immediate sign of excitement—that our bodies are preparing for the event?

It's understandable if you have played badly in the past because of nerves and tension, why would you think it's a good thing in the moment? Again, when you realize that your thoughts and the adrenaline are just part of the fight/flight response—developed thousands of years ago out of our need to survive—you might not be as alarmed when you tense up. Instead of nerves being a sign of weakness or potential failure, they become something to manage and, ultimately, master. It's not that you always choke under pressure or that you're not good enough. The problem has been your reaction to the nerves themselves.

How about we put this into action in real life? You have an important event coming up, and you're stressed about it. You are trapped in an anxious maze of thoughts, and you start to feel these uncomfortable physical sensations in your body. You also wonder, *"What's going to happen this weekend? I hope I play okay."*

You could be anywhere when all of this starts kicking in—the shower, lying in bed, or on the car ride home from practice the night before the event. It doesn't matter. Wherever you are, when you're starting to feel uneasy, you remind yourself that you are in charge of what you think and feel about the upcoming event. So, you choose to be excited. You accept this opportunity to work on your reaction to the nerves, and you return to the mastery mindset.

Once you reframe what's happening and adjust your perspective, you shift your attention to the sensation of the water on your back in the shower, or you feel the bed or car seat supporting you. Focusing on sensation (not thinking in your head) will interrupt your thoughts. Then, you decide to either visualize performing well or you pick a different topic to think about. Another good option is to begin taking deeper breaths, which will calm your nervous system. Know that the remote control is in your hand. You just need to start pressing these buttons.

Michael Jordan loved these physical feelings before games so much that he actually said, "The day I don't feel butterflies in my stomach is the day I'm going to quit basketball." Michael still seeks out pressure wherever he can, especially on the golf course these days. He loves it. But learning to embrace and eventually love this feeling takes effort at first.

Here is a conversation with one of my clients I think you'll relate to:

"How's your anxiety been lately?" I ask.

"It's been overwhelming at times," he admits.

"I understand. That adrenaline comes on quickly, doesn't it?" I acknowledge.

"Yeah. Sometimes I can focus well even when I feel it, but other times, it feels like the nerves just take over."

"That's true," I say. "When we feel some adrenaline, it can help us play better. But when the nerves are more intense, we need to pause, take a deep breath, and not get pulled into the negative loop. We don't need to get rid of this feeling. We actually need a certain amount of adrenaline to play our best. Think about it. If the adrenaline is too low, we would get bored and play worse."

"I never thought of it this way," he acknowledges. "Most of the time, I get anxious when I feel the adrenaline and assume things are going to go downhill. I never thought it could help me."

Once you become more comfortable accepting or even embracing these nerves, it can become the main ingredient to your best performances. This may seem like a stretch right now, but it's true.

It's time to experience nerves as a source of power and potential. When you feel those butterflies fluttering in your stomach, instead of bracing for the worst—love this experience. Be grateful for the adrenaline pumping in your blood. Then, refocus on your intentions and commit.

When you do, there is no limit to what you can achieve.

17

Train Yourself to Be Loose

IN THE LAST CHAPTER, "Create a New Relationship with Your Nerves," you were introduced to the idea of accepting your nerves as a source of natural energy to use and not resist.

Now, we need to deal with the physical tension that frequently comes with feeling nervous. Think of physical tightness as energy that gets trapped inside of you—like air in a pipe. It's difficult to know what to do with this feeling, especially when we're in the heat of battle.

First, your goal in this situation is to drop into a looser state, not to relax. Being relaxed isn't helpful or realistic when it comes to optimal performance. When you notice that you are tight, you can learn to let go of it and refocus on the task at hand.

Even dropping just a little tension can improve your performance and increase your confidence immediately.

I remember the first moment when being loose became a thing.

I'm playing a tennis match and my opponent's serve is clocking in at—get this—130 mph! How can I not tense up, seeing these bullets whiz by me as I assess my chances of winning? But instead of seeing my only path to victory being an injury to his shoulder, I decide to surrender and let go of the tension in my body. Since I'm not worrying about the tension anymore, I can focus my attention on the ball. I make clean contact on his next serve as I release the energy in my arms and allow my entire body to go forward, without holding back. My return blazes crosscourt at about 100 mph for a winner.

"*That is weird,*" I think to myself. I just couldn't believe how fluid I was feeling and how hard I was hitting the ball. Not being in my head is also new. I trust my body and let the energy or adrenaline channel through me. I don't feel relaxed, but my body is loose. Zero tension. Of course, I decide to stick with this "no-mind"/loose body approach and end up winning the match in straight sets.

A few weeks later, in another important match for my club, I was able to do this again. This experience was a new mind-body state, a totally different dimension. "*This is really cool,*" I thought to myself.

Learning to drop tension and perform with looser muscles requires experimenting and practice. You need to experience this for yourself. Because we tend to overcontrol so much, it requires a new level of trust and curiosity.

But once you feel this looseness, you can train it in practice. How? By contrasting the difference between tight and loose.

One popular technique is called the "body scan" (i.e., taking a mental x-ray of a specific body part). For instance, instead of being in your head and judging your last shot or move, use your remote control to change the channel and locate where in your body you feel tension. It's usually in the upper body. Your legs might feel heavy, too, but being loose is most helpful when you release your arms and hands in a more elastic way—a little bit like a rubber band.

In your next practice, see if you can feel what I'm talking about. If you're shooting a basketball, release the ball off your fingertips. Feel the sensation. If you are at the plate taking batting practice, let your upper body swing more freely. If you are throwing a ball, allow your shoulders and hand to release the ball without trying to control it. Your arms are elastic, you feel fluid—it's the opposite of being tight and restricted, which happens when we tense up, feel scared to make a mistake, and don't trust our body. Notice the difference. It is this contrast between the two that will give you access to this physical feeling in competition.

The exciting thing is that you can train yourself to produce this feeling in practice every day. I got lucky and randomly discovered it when I was twenty-six, but you can learn it now.

With practice, you will be able to drop into a looser state simply by recalling the feeling, which will become muscle memory. It's not a thought, it's a physical feeling.

There is a natural tendency to muscle our way through things when we feel tight, forcing our moves rather than letting them happen. It's essential to resist this urge to control your body. When you feel like holding back or tensing up, do the opposite—let it go. When you are aware of these moments and choose to trust your body, despite having doubts, you will be exercising your personal power, which will increase your confidence in a big way.

The biggest mental trap that can prevent you from building this "looseness" into your sport in the big moments, when you're under pressure, is believing that you will make a mistake *because* you feel tight. You may feel tight but you don't have to perform tight. This is a *choice*. Remember, act how you want to feel.

> You've got to be loose. You've got to be loose enough so that the ball just flows out of your hand. You can't be tight and worried about being perfect. You have to trust your mechanics and let it go.
> —Sandy Koufax, baseball pitcher, Hall of Famer

You no longer need to get stuck in this tension—playing it safe, hoping you can somehow escape with a win anyway, or bracing against mistakes. By tuning into your body and releasing the stored tension, you will be tapping into the same physical state that the best athletes in the world rely on.

18

Center Your Mind

I HOPE IT'S STARTING to sink in that your mind is more powerful than you realize. In Chapter 11, we explored two aspects of focus—internal and external—and three dimensions of time (past, present, and future). This is important to keep in mind as we continue to build your "inner remote control." But the main thing for now is that you understand you can change the channel any time you need to. Centering is another important button on the remote that will help you return to the present moment.

If someone had ever told me that I could purposely shift my attention or "center" my mind (i.e., literally stop my thoughts, forget the score, drop my anger after the last horrible error), I would have assumed they were either messing with me or that they were on drugs.

Without a doubt, this is another skill that I would hand to my younger self if I could turn the clock back. But even better, you get to learn it now.

Try to imagine having an elevator in your brain, allowing your focus to drop out of your head and away from all your thoughts in a split second. That's what this centering technique does. As you learned in the last chapter, "Train Yourself to Be Loose," this is a shift of focus from thoughts to a focus within your body, where there is no thinking.

Go ahead and try this now. Drop your attention into your core, just above your belly button. This is the mid-point of your body, hence the name "centering." For now, simply recognize that you changed the channel again, and be aware of the difference between being in your head and switching your focus to somewhere in your body. Add a deep breath if you like, and for the entire breath, focus your attention on your belly button.

Now, let's do something fun. Think of a negative thought that comes up during a challenging moment in an event, such as *"That was a bad error."* Or *"Coach is going to be mad."* Or *"I can't make another mistake."* It can be any thought you want, but not too short or too long for this exercise. Do you have a thought ready? In a moment, I'm going to have you repeat this thought again to yourself silently, up to five times. Then, whenever you choose, drop your focus into your core and *feel*—not think about—your stomach around your belly button for a few seconds—the center of your body. Okay. Take the thought now and repeat it in your head and then drop your attention at any point.

What happened to your thought when you shifted your focus to your core? It should have disappeared. If you perform this exercise correctly and shift your focus as I described, the thought in your head will vanish. If that didn't happen, do it again by feeling the spot around your belly button. Sometimes people *think* about their core—the idea of the belly button— but they're not feeling the sensation of it, which is completely different.

In fact, any time you feel a sensation in your body (your feet touching the ground, your fingers on the computer or resting on your lap, etc.), you cannot be thinking a thought at the same time. If you grasp this concept and practice doing this throughout your day, it can be a great way to get out of your head for a few seconds and will serve as a helpful reset button for you.

The late Kobe Bryant shared his insights on resetting amidst the storm:

> The game is full of ebbs and flows—the good, the bad, and everything in between. With all that was happening around me, I had to figure out how to still my mind and stay calm and centered. My emotions did spike and drop at times, but I was aware enough to recalibrate and bring them back in line before things spiraled out of control. I could do that in a way others couldn't, and that was really key for me.
> —Kobe Bryant, *Mamba Mentality* (page 175)

An essential part of developing mental toughness is being able to drop out of your head when you find yourself overthinking. When your coaches yell, "Get your head in the game," or "You've got to think out there," it may be confusing. Think more? But often these commands lead to paralysis. What your coaches are really saying is that they want you to focus on the right things and not give in to the distractions, including your thoughts.

When practicing this centering technique, you might notice that whatever thoughts occupied your mind before you started may come rushing back after doing it. This is normal. It takes a little practice to get the hang of it. I recommend doing this a couple of times each day to practice this technique. Take a moment to let go of your thoughts by dropping into your core, or by feeling the bottoms of your feet touching the ground when you walk (a favorite)—whether you're on your way to practice, between classes, or even at home, walking around from time to time. You'll likely appreciate this mental break.

Centering your mind will help you effortlessly reset and become present, allowing you to fully engage in the battle at hand.

19

Breathe with Intention

JUST FOR A MOMENT, I want you to visualize your classroom at school. Then, double it to two classrooms. Now picture three thousand one-gallon milk cartons lined up, covering the entire floor of both classrooms. Got it? That is how much air you breathe in and out each day!

Listen, by now, I bet a coach, teacher, or parent has suggested you take a deep breath when they see you getting nervous or frustrated. Maybe you've also tried taking a deep breath in tough moments, but it didn't do much for you.

I understand that expecting a few deep breaths to solve all your problems in the heat of battle sounds like a long shot. I remember thinking this when I first learned about this technique. "*I already know how to breathe,*" I thought to myself. "*How is this supposed to help anything?*" But if almost every Olympic athlete uses deep breathing, there has to be more to the story, right? Imagine training for the Olympics for four years, facing that kind of immense pressure as you pursue a gold medal. I imagine you would also want a foolproof way to stay calm.

Just know that if using the deep breath hasn't been working for you, there are reasons for this, which you'll discover shortly. I want you to know that the deep, diaphragmatic breath can become one of your most powerful weapons.

Why is the right kind of breath helpful? We happen to be the most advanced species on the planet—even if this doesn't seem to be the case these days—given our remarkable ability to think ahead and use our imagination. As a result, we have complex thoughts, feelings, and a delicate nervous system.

As you may recall, since our brain is strongly wired to keep us alive, it will also be on the lookout for anything that might be a threat. Thousands of years ago, this was a disease or a stray animal. When we bring this human skill into the sports arena, the threat becomes playing badly, losing, and the fear of people rejecting you.

This is where the deep breath comes in. If you do this correctly, it is the most natural way to calm your entire nervous system and let go of thoughts. It will immediately increase oxygen (O_2) in your brain and kick in what we call the "relaxation response." It will also help you focus and refocus.

The key to this technique is to breathe deeply from your stomach, not directly from your chest. Most people do this incorrectly because they are trying to "perform" the breath, which feels forced. But when you breathe in deeply and slowly through your nose and exhale slowly out of your mouth, your brain will get the message that things are okay—that you are safe. However, if the breaths happen to be short and come from the chest, your brain will think you are in trouble.

If you fully commit to this practice and use it even when you're not competing, you will see why this is so helpful. When you put it together with the centering technique you just learned, it's a winning combination.

All successful athletes and performers use deep breathing constantly. Steph Curry is the NBA's most valuable player and uses breathing and meditation to help him stay alert by coming back to the present moment. He views breathing as a crucial skill, not just for recovery and controlling nerves, but for overall performance. He has been actively working on mastering breathing techniques, particularly diaphragmatic breathing, in his training regimen.

Another well-known example is Novak Djokovic, the Serbian twenty-five-time Grand Slam champion. Djokovic is renowned for his meticulous focus on physical and mental preparation, and breathing techniques have been a main part of his routine. He has credited intentional breathing exercises as a significant factor in improving his stamina, focus, and mental clarity during matches. He practices mindfulness and yoga, using deep breathing to maintain his composure, especially in high-pressure situations.

One notable moment was during the 2019 Wimbledon final against Roger Federer. The match was intense, lasting nearly five hours, and became the longest singles final in Wimbledon history. Djokovic faced two championship points but managed to stay calm and composed, a feat he attributes in large part to his breathing techniques. He won the match.

By practicing controlled breathing, Djokovic has been able to control his heart rate, stay focused, and manage high levels of stress better than most of his competitors since he started using this technique.

Intentional breathing helps Djokovic not only in matches but also in recovery and everyday life, contributing to his longevity and success in the sport.

Breath Training Plan

Sit or lie down in a quiet setting where you won't be distracted. Give yourself permission to practice this for a few minutes. Be curious about it.

Take three deep breaths and notice what is rising more—your stomach or your chest.

Put one hand on your chest and one hand on your stomach. Imagine taking a nap to avoid overperforming it. As you inhale, imagine blowing up a balloon in your stomach. Your bottom hand will rise if you are doing it correctly.

Once you get the hang of this, take six deep breaths for about one minute (taking four seconds to breathe in, one second to hold, and six seconds to exhale).

Notice how you feel compared to how you felt a few minutes prior to the breathing practice.

If you're motivated, do this once per day for the next two weeks. Repeat as much as you like. Initially, you may notice that the hand on your chest rises more than the hand on your stomach, which is completely normal. Try to avoid the urge for perfection. Instead, stay curious and simply observe which hand is rising more.

If your stomach does not rise much (indicating more chest breathing), again, pretend you are taking a nap. If the idea of napping doesn't make sense to you, purposely push your stomach out as you breathe in through your nose to feel your diaphragm rise.

If you begin using this outside of competition—in school, on car rides to games, while doing homework, or in bed before sleep—you will turn this skill into a weapon that you can use for the rest of your life in tough moments. Breathing deeply usually won't fully erase your nerves and adrenaline immediately in competition, but it will calm you down increasingly when you need it most. When you breathe deeply to return to the present moment, simply because it feels comforting and pleasurable to you—not only because you hope it removes whatever negativity you may be experiencing—you will benefit greatly from intentional breathing. Nerves, tension, and frustration are all a natural part of being a competitive athlete, and using the deep breath will help unleash your inner warrior.

20

Make Adjustments Like the Pros

THERE'S ANOTHER COMMON MENTAL trap you may have fallen into without realizing it. This trap has to do with overthinking your technique and telling yourself how to move: *"Stay down." "Don't open the face so much." "Choke up." "Don't pull off the ball."* I know it is tempting to want to correct every mistake immediately, but this approach isn't always beneficial. In fact, overthinking your moves might be the main reason you've been struggling. Even when your technique is a little off, if you think too much, you will probably just doubt yourself even more.

There is an exception to this —having a single "cue" or "swing thought" (i.e., forward, up, through, finish) can be helpful, provided you stay committed to executing it without second-guessing. You also don't want to have more than one "cue" or image. The more thoughts you have, the less effective, and maybe even harmful, they will be to your performance.

Jonny Mosley, the 1998 Olympic gold medalist in moguls, found these "cues" extremely helpful in tough moments when he raced. "I always get nervous. . . . Being too flat or over-amped was always an issue in bumps." During his runs, he relied on intense mental focus—carrying a small slip of paper in his pocket that listed cues like "hands" and "weight over the outside ski." Whenever his mind raced, he'd pull it out and repeat: "I can do that." This simple ritual helped him recenter on the fundamentals and also calm his nerves.

If you have been executing your skills consistently in practice, then it's obvious it isn't a technical problem you're having in competition. It's a "state of being" problem—feeling too tense, hesitating out of fear of making a mistake, forcing the move, or doubting yourself at the last second. As I said in the introduction of the book, the idea that our mental and physical state can affect our technique did not even occur to me when I was young.

Recently, I spoke with a seventeen-year-old soccer player who recognized how she would never think about her skills in competition when she was playing well, even if she made a mistake. But she acknowledged overthinking mistakes when she wasn't happy with her performance. She told me that she didn't know what else to do.

During our meeting, I asked her, "When you're playing well, how do you deal with a mistake?"

"Sometimes I think about different tactical plays, but my adjustments feel pretty automatic," she replied. "I get into a kind of zone, and mistakes don't really bother me. I don't feel the need to correct them in the same way. I trust my body and feel confident that I'll just make the next shot."

"Do your adjustments change when you're having an off day?" I inquired.

"Yeah, they definitely do," she admitted. "I get much more technical and start overthinking."

"How does that usually play out for you?" I asked.

"Usually, not very well. When the first adjustment doesn't work, I try another one or maybe even two, but when they don't work, I get really frustrated," she confessed.

"It sounds like your intuition is telling you not to worry about these errors when you're playing well," I pointed out. "Staying present in your body—playing from 'downstairs'—is often a better response than going 'upstairs' into your head to fix a mistake."

"Yes, for sure." She laughed. "I just thought I always had to fix my mistakes. I didn't realize there was another way to handle it."

In competition, focusing less on technique and adjusting your focus, muscle tension, and intensity levels can be much more effective. You can also utilize images in your mind instead of thinking. For example, if you tend to rush or make impulsive moves, take a moment to visualize the correct movement. Picture the pass spiraling into the receiver's hands or the ball sinking into the basket. This visualization should be a quick one- to two-second image, rather than a stream of thoughts or tips. Using visualization can accelerate your learning and is usually more effective, as you learned in Chapter 14, "Visualize Before and During Competition." It's also extremely helpful to exaggerate the correct movement—doing it more than you think you need to. This can be a game-changer when it comes to handling mistakes—correct from your body or a visual, and then exaggerate the motion.

When you trust your adjustments, you'll also be able to accept your mistakes more quickly, allowing you to stay focused on what truly matters—the mastery mindset, your targets, and your tactical plan.

For instance, do you notice when you're rushing, leaning back too much, hesitating at the point of execution, or becoming unfocused while worrying about the consequences of the match or game? This awareness—there's that word again—will help you stay present long enough to use your muscle memory and find the right "cues" to make the adjustment.

It's also helpful to know that you have just about one second after a mistake to truly feel the sensation in your body, which will help you choose the best adjustment (hint: it should be very simple and easy to execute). By staying calm, physically present, and out of your head, you'll be able to make an adjustment like a professional athlete—by slowing things down, choosing your next move with intention, and releasing your body with greater trust. These quick and simple adjustments will always be personal to you. But when you commit and exaggerate the move with your body, not your thoughts, it will make all the difference.

SECTION 5

Emotional Intelligence & Communication

PEAK PERFORMANCE DOESN'T HAPPEN in isolation.

This section helps you understand and express emotions in ways that fuel—not sabotage—your performance. You'll also learn how to set boundaries, give and receive feedback, and navigate relationships with teammates, coaches, and family.

Mental toughness includes emotional maturity. When you understand your emotions and communicate effectively, you perform more freely, handle conflict better, and lead with clarity and integrity.

In this section, you'll learn how to:

- Stay grounded under pressure or conflict.
- Express yourself clearly and assertively.
- Use gratitude and emotional insight to build team connection.

21

Compete with Gratitude

I HOPE YOU ARE starting to feel more self-mastery as you continue to install the buttons on your inner remote control. As your confidence grows, you will find a new headspace that gives you a little more freedom to appreciate your sport and the competition even more.

This is where gratitude can become your greatest ally. You may be thinking, *"Oh, yeah. I hear this from my parents all the time, usually on Thanksgiving."* But I'm not talking about something you do one day a year.

No. I'm referring to a state of mind that allows you to be fully present and deeply appreciative of the moment at hand, even after making a mistake in a big moment. It is a deeper understanding that you are fortunate to be competing at all—that you have this special opportunity to put yourself on the line and can appreciate these adrenaline-filled moments. With this broader perspective—part of the mastery mindset you're building—you can enjoy your sport, without results being your only metric of success.

You might think that professional sports would be the last place to find a mindset of gratitude, given everything that's at stake for these elite athletes. Consider LeBron James: Despite facing numerous challenges throughout his life—being born to a sixteen-year-old mother, frequently moving from one apartment to another, and growing up without a father figure—he remains grateful for the game and the support of those around him. LeBron's upbringing in tough neighborhoods was compounded by his mother, Gloria's, struggles to find stable employment. Yet, he hasn't forgotten to express gratitude for the game and the people who have positively influenced his life. He even established the LeBron James Family Foundation to give back to children and families facing similar hardships. One of the foundation's slogans, "Just a kid from Akron," perfectly encapsulates how LeBron stays humble and views his success through a lens of gratitude. He also practices meditation to maintain this positive mindset.

When you feel grateful, something really cool happens in your brain. The amygdala, a small almond-shaped part of the brain responsible for your emotions (including fear), lights up. As you probably know, too much emotion is not helpful when you are trying to execute. But remembering to appreciate the moment, especially stressful ones, will calm your mind instantly.

There's a simple way to unlock this skill right now. Please close your eyes and take a few moments and visualize those thrilling moments you've experienced in your sport. See this in your mind. It's okay if the images aren't that clear at first. Just relax and reflect on a time when you were having fun and loving the competition. Maybe you want to picture your coach, your parents, and your friends cheering for you on the sidelines. Think about how fortunate you were to be competing at all. Not everyone gets this opportunity—not by a long shot. Imagine the power you feel with the ball in your hands, the rush of adrenaline as you sprint down the field, the triumph you feel when you win, and the joy of sharing these special moments with your teammates and family.

Wasn't it exhilarating to be in the mix, handling pressure, and striving for a win? Recognize that there are incredible moments to appreciate, even if they don't always lead to victory. This mindset is vastly different from worrying about failing, obsessing over past errors, or getting caught up in bad calls by referees.

I understand that shifting into a state of gratitude—reflecting on what you appreciate, even after a tough loss or missing a crucial shot—is easier said than done. That's why you must keep this concept in the front of your mind, especially on game day. Begin appreciating the little wins—moments when you chose to be aggressive or when you were able to let go of errors and reset. Bring your best mental effort every single day.

Learn the lessons from your inevitable and painful setbacks. Celebrate your progress even if you haven't reached all your goals yet. There will always be more you can do. So, do your best to appreciate right now, even if you're in a hard place. This pain can be the very thing you need to help you finally commit to the mastery mindset.

Before your event, take a moment and remind yourself to enjoy the upcoming battle, even as the butterflies drop in for a visit, which they most certainly will. This pre-event time will help you shift your mindset, allowing you to feel satisfied not solely in the outcome but in the experience itself.

As hard as it is, when you get frustrated, remember that you're lucky to be out there. There will be many more opportunities to prove yourself. Gratitude will also reduce your nerves and remove your frustration when you make an error, as it is impossible to be angry and grateful at the same time.

As you develop this deep level of mental toughness, draw inspiration from LeBron James and other accomplished athletes who harness this special state of mind. Cherish every moment spent playing your sport, and express appreciation for your parents and coaches. When you approach your athletic journey with gratitude, you transform not only your experience but also the way you engage with the competition.

Isn't it motivating to know there's real science behind the experience of gratitude? I hope this inspires you to stop in the middle of the action next time and remember why you are playing your sport—because you love to compete.

Like LeBron, you, too, can approach competition with gratitude in the front of your mind.

22

Assert Yourself

Do YOU EVER FEEL like people sometimes get a little too involved in your life—in your academics and your sport?

Maybe your coach yells at you to get your head in the game and fix something, which only makes you feel more worried?

What about your teammates? Do they ride you when you make a costly error under pressure?

It's almost a guarantee that you will find yourself feeling annoyed at times during your competitive sports journey—with your parents, your coaches, and your teammates.

I understand how irritating and demoralizing this can feel. By now, you may be quite sick of it but unsure what you can do about it. Maybe you think to yourself, *"Will my parents even listen if I tell them how much it bothers me when they lecture me in the car after the game? It'll probably just make it worse."*

Sure, you could say nothing and just hope it goes away. You could also just pretend you're listening when they start talking to you. Maybe you've already mastered this—where you nod your head like you're listening or say, "Uh-huh," and they just keep on talking.

However, as frustrating as this can be, neither your parents nor your coach are trying to make you feel bad, even if it feels that way. It may be hard to believe sometimes, but they aren't intending to make your life more miserable. It's usually the exact opposite. They want you to work hard, improve, and have sports be a stepping stone for the future. Yes, they want you to win, too. They want this for you, and they also want it for themselves, which is where it can get a little dicey, I know. When you play well and win, it feels good for everyone.

It's frustrating when parents and coaches add pressure without realizing it. The expectations can be overwhelming.

I experienced this first-hand with my daughter, Ally, a talented, three-sport athlete (soccer, track, and cross-country) in high school. I just loved watching her compete. Her hand-eye coordination was off the charts. I remember pitching tennis balls to her when she was three years old, and she would make perfect contact on almost every pitch. She also had such grit and tenacity, which became obvious very early.

One evening during dinner, I turned to her, knowing she had a track meet coming up, and said, "We can't wait to watch you run this weekend."

I was stunned by what came next: "I don't want you or Mom to come," she said.

"What do you mean?" I shot back.

"It's my sport, not yours, and I don't want you to come."

She was never one to sugar-coat her feelings. At two years old, she actually pushed my hand away when I was trying to help put her shirt on and said, "Me do it." She was strong-willed and independent from the starting blocks, which I've always admired about her.

But to be honest, in that moment, I didn't know what to say after she banned us from her sports events. I was caught between what I wanted and this new revelation that she didn't want the same thing.

What was so difficult, even painful, was that I actually worked with parents and coaches to help them take the pressure off their kids. So, it was really difficult for me to hear.

What was I supposed to do?

My daughter had a point, didn't she? It was her sport, not mine. But I loved watching her run for the ball in soccer and pick off people when she ran the 800, which was her main track event. Did I like seeing her run well and win? Of course. But I mainly loved just seeing her determination and passion to compete.

Also, I thought, *"What about all the other parents who weren't banned by their kids? Why me, of all people?"*

This is where the road gets twisty, though. Yes, I could have been forceful and told my daughter that I was going to come anyway, and that she had to deal with it. But that's not my nature. I asked her why she didn't want us to come, but she just repeated her position about it being her sport and not ours.

In the end, we chose to honor her feelings. We gave her this space to compete without the extra pressure.

I know all too well that even if parents don't think they're adding pressure, they do just by their presence. It's always a mixed bag, isn't it? If you're playing well, you probably want them there. But you might not when you have an off day.

In the case with my daughter, she asserted herself—just like she always had. I wish she could have known my true feelings about just loving the experience of watching, without judgment, but that's not how she felt about it.

So, admittedly, even though I honored her wish, I did sneak into a few of her races without her knowing. I cherished those moments, but they were also nerve-racking because I was ducking a lot so she wouldn't see me.

I've always been proud of her for speaking her mind, and I've done my best to listen to and honor both of my kids' feelings. They matter to me.

Sometimes parents forget how important it is to give you a chance to make your own choices—not because they don't care, but because they care too much. But not always in the most helpful way.

Speaking your mind isn't easy. But it can also pay off.

I recently worked with a young basketball player named Sean who is being recruited by several top schools, including Stanford University. However, in the past six months, Sean started to struggle. He was in a slump. When his parents called me, they explained how Sean's coach was really getting to him. But instead of facing his coach, Sean began beating himself up after mistakes. Fortunately, he wanted to understand why this was happening. He didn't make the connection between his anger and his coach's criticism.

> Coach goes hard at me a lot. He says he sees a lot of potential and wants to push me to be my best. He believes if he doesn't do it, no one else will. But for me, that approach has never worked. It just makes me lose confidence. It seems that every mistake is like I'm losing a national championship.

Once Sean realized that it was the coach's anger that was bothering him, he decided to talk to him directly. Even so, Sean was worried about how his coach would react. But he also recognized that it was an opportunity to assert himself. He felt it was a risk worth taking, and it paid off. The coach was not only impressed with Sean's courage to talk about it, he also became more positive in games and stopped yelling at him.

This is why I want to encourage you to learn to speak up and coach them so they understand what you need. I understand it's not easy to do. But this is an important opportunity for you. I promise you that being able to communicate your needs will come in handy down the road.

I know it's tempting to avoid uncomfortable conversations. It is easier to "suck it up," as my father used to say when I got upset after a loss. It seems easier to ignore our feelings than to face them.

Even though your parents and coaches support you and want you to excel, remember they aren't perfect. It seems like parents and coaches *should* know how their comments will affect you, but sometimes they don't. When they remind you to jump rope because the coach said you needed to be in a little better cardio shape, they think they are doing the right thing.

But you might think to yourself, *"Why can't my parents see how annoying it is to talk about the importance of the upcoming tournament? Don't they know that comparing me to my siblings and teammates makes me feel worse?"*

I'm a parent of two teenagers and a leading expert in performance psychology. My job is to understand how the mind works and how families can build healthier relationships. And yet, I still make dumb mistakes as a parent, as my son would gladly tell you. For example, I used to stretch when he was playing a tennis match or when he was pitching in a Little League game because I was hoping he would think that I wasn't *that* into it. I was actually trying to take the pressure off him.

But of course, my behavior irritated him more, and it did the opposite. He wasn't shy to tell me, and I was relieved he did. My intentions were right. My execution wasn't. He coached me, and I learned from it. I want you to find the courage and the words so you can express yourself, too. You have every right to share how you feel. You can also do this without making anyone wrong by expressing how you feel, not giving them your opinion about their choices.

Let's knock down the walls that stop you from being assertive with your parents, your coaches, or your teammates. The first barrier is the assumption you're likely making: that speaking up won't do anything; that there's no point because they won't change; or that it will only make things worse. What if the thought was, instead, something like: *"Maybe telling them won't change anything. But at least I can take some control back. If something bothers me, I have the right to express myself, regardless of what they decide to do. I can't control what they do, but I can let them know what helps me and what doesn't."*

I understand if this is difficult to imagine right now. But parents and coaches need to know how you feel. If they say something that feels like extra pressure, tell them. If you do, it will give you more confidence and a feeling of independence, which is important for your development. It will also contribute to better performances.

Becoming mentally tough means taking responsibility for your own needs and clearly communicating what helps you grow—especially in your relationships. When you do, you will be rewarded both on and off the field.

23

Engage with Controlled Aggression

It's COMMON KNOWLEDGE THAT being aggressive is usually the best approach, regardless of the sport. But this is easier said than done, isn't it? Perhaps you tried to be more aggressive in one of your recent events, but you got chewed out because it was reckless. Or maybe you did it at the wrong time. You might also feel that being aggressive, especially after an error, isn't the smartest move.

Your challenge is to find the right balance of what I call "controlled aggression." You don't want to play it too safe, but being reckless can be just as detrimental—in the short term. When trying something new, it's common to swing to extremes—being overly aggressive one moment and then too timid the next.

But how can you find this balance if you keep backing down every time you make a mistake? I understand how tempting it is to take your foot off the gas pedal just a little because you worry about making a mistake. For instance, let's say you're on the eighteenth hole, and if you sink this putt, you know you'll win the round. Or maybe there are just a few minutes left in the game, and your team desperately needs a goal to tie. In those moments, you know the outcome rests on your next move. Unfortunately, at the last second, you back off and miss out on the opportunity or make a costly error.

The truth is, in sports and in life, you will always feel better about your performance and yourself when you lean into the moment—by taking the shot, swinging through the ball, going for the steal, picking your receiver, jumping off the diving board, or sticking the landing. Even if you don't succeed on a particular day, you can build on this mentality. You will always get more chances to adjust and make better choices next time. So, let's move the needle toward *more aggressive* as opposed to *playing it safe*.

One of my clients, a pro tennis player on the ATP Tour, won the biggest junior national tournament in the US a few years ago. He became the number one player in the United States by being consistent and defending well. He was so good playing this way that he never pushed himself to develop an aggressive mentality—an essential mindset at the highest levels of sports.

It has taken more than two years on the pro tour to get him mentally prepared to step up and genuinely unleash his shots without reverting to a more defensive style. Gradually, he's making progress, moving up one hundred spots in the rankings over the past few months. He's now earning a respectable income by playing tennis. However, he acknowledges that if he had developed this level of aggression when he was younger, he would have been in a much better position when he turned pro. The earlier you can commit to being aggressive, the more success you will have down the road.

Even if you're not planning to play your sport professionally, choosing to be more aggressive—especially when self-doubt creeps in—will help you move closer to your goals. It may feel risky now, but it's a smart investment.

I understand it can be hard sometimes to be aggressive, especially when you're frustrated. But to make progress with this goal, it's important not to let your emotions get in the way. This is why I wrote this book for you—so you can execute in these difficult moments with a mastery mindset.

There will be times when you play it safe, and that's okay. Just keep noticing your actions and recommit to being aggressive.

You get to choose your mental approach in your sport and in life, even if it doesn't always feel like you do. When you choose to perform with controlled aggression, it will boost your confidence, lead to more consistent performances, help you secure more wins, and ultimately allow you to experience the deepest sense of self-satisfaction possible.

24

Channel Your Anger

IMAGINE YOU HAVE ONE of your most important high school races or championship games coming up. Knowing your father tends to be loud and distracting at events, you decide to take the extra precaution of asking him to keep it down—although that's no easy task.

You find him right before the coach gathers the team and say, "Dad, it's great you're here, but can you please just stay calm and not yell from the sidelines today?"

"Of course, son," he assures you. "I'll zip it. You won't hear a peep from me."

Relieved, you can now focus on the game without worrying about distractions. But not even thirty minutes in, you catch a glimpse of your dad in the stands, standing up and yelling your name as loud as he can after you save a goal for the team, "You've got this, Jack!"

How do you think you might feel? Angry? Embarrassed?

This exact scenario happened to me during the finals of my second World Championships in 2012. I was furious. Despite all the strategies and tools I had learned in my lifetime, I felt completely overwhelmed, and I admit that I lost my cool.

I was winning the match until the moment my dad stood up and shouted my name. Within minutes, I found myself trailing 1–4 in the second set. Amidst the anxiety and adrenaline racing through me, I remember glaring over at my dad and pointing to my pounding heart in anger as if to say, "This is your fault." I was immersed in my frustration and blamed him for everything that was happening to me in that moment.

Of course, as you now know, we can never blame anyone for our feelings. We are in charge of our reactions. Standing up and yelling was not helpful, to say the least. But how I chose to react was 100 percent on me.

My reaction wasn't good. But my thoughts were even worse: *"I'm going to lose the World Championships now,"* I thought to myself. *"I can't believe this is happening."*

With the momentum now completely against me, my rational brain kicked in. I was still fuming, but at least I was aware of it. Given the nerves and high level of adrenaline I was feeling, I realized I had to do something different.

In a daze, I walked to the back fence surrounding the court and centered my mind in my naval to reset. However, I quickly realized that my adrenaline was running so high that this would not be enough in this situation. This is where awareness helps. Knowing how you feel and what you might need in a certain moment allows you to choose which button to hit on the remote.

So, I took a few deep breaths. This helped a little, but not as much as I wished. With this emotional tsunami raging inside of me, I realized that I had only one choice left—to use the same strategy that helps with muscle tension—and I decided to channel all my frustration and anger into my shots.

I walked decisively from the back fence to the baseline to return serve, feeling a surge of determination. The adrenaline was still there, but I suddenly felt more in control of it. My focus narrowed on the ball. I was locked in and now committed to unleashing my shots, regardless of how I felt. First shot, winner. Next point, same thing: winner. My opponent wasn't even in striking distance. This decisiveness, combined with my narrow focus, completely shifted my state and feeling of momentum. My opponent didn't win another game. I averted disaster and secured my second World Championship in straight sets.

Not surprisingly, after the match, feeling relieved and holding the trophy, I cracked a smile at my dad, who was beaming from ear to ear in the stands. With a fresh perspective, free from the adrenaline that had hijacked me during the match, I couldn't help but think, *"What is he supposed to do? He cares about me. It's actually pretty cool he got to witness that."* It's not like my dad was trying to make me lose. He was my biggest fan. But as you know, in the moment, it's not easy to recognize this, is it?

Was there a situation in one of your events when emotions got the best of you, too? What would it have looked like for you to channel your anger instead of letting it take you down? Mine almost did. Awareness helped a lot.

In the heat of battle, especially when dealing with nervous energy, frustration, or anger, there comes a point when it may be more effective to use those emotions rather than trying to stop them. Many athletes use this strategy, understanding that releasing emotion can transform it into positive energy. However, like any technique, it needs to be applied at the right time. As Michael Jordan puts it, "Use your anger as a tool, not as a weapon."

LeBron James shares a similar perspective: "I used to let anger define me; now, I use it to drive my intensity and passion on the court."

Instead of letting anger control you, know that it can be harnessed to enhance your focus and level of commitment when you're feeling overwhelmed.

So, if you find yourself boiling over and you can't calm down, consider tapping into this channeling strategy for yourself. Don't hold back. Release the ball off your fingertips without hesitation, let the adrenaline flow from your heart to your legs, and propel yourself uphill. Use your intensity to go head-to-head, steal the ball, or swing at a pitch near the plate with full confidence that it's going exactly where you intended.

The emotions that surface in competition can work for you or against you. Now you know there's a better option than letting it set you on fire and ruin your performance. You can experience this same satisfaction when you choose to turn your negative emotions into something positive and productive.

25

Take Advantage of Your Injury

THE STORY OF THOMAS MUSTER, formerly ranked number one in the world on the pro tennis tour, is one of incredible perseverance and resilience. In 1989, after reaching the finals of the Miami Open, Muster was hit by a drunk driver shortly before the finals, causing severe damage to his left knee. It was a devastating moment, as the injury was so severe that many thought it might end his career.

However, Muster's determination proved stronger. He underwent surgery and embarked on an intense rehabilitation process. Remarkably, within just six months, he was back on the court, using his strong work ethic and mental strength to not only return to the game but also excel.

By 1995, Muster achieved a tremendous comeback by reaching the pinnacle of success. He claimed the number one spot in the world and won the French Open that year. His tenacity and relentless spirit, despite the physical and mental challenges posed by the accident, became a powerful inspiration to athletes around the world.

If you've ever been injured, you know the mental challenges: being out of your sport for weeks or months, losing your conditioning, enduring the monotony of rehabilitation, and fighting depression from a lack of activity, on top of worrying about re-injury and the possibility of not reaching your old level.

Getting injured can be one of the most difficult experiences to deal with in competitive sports. It immediately takes you out of commission and destroys your confidence instantly. But you have a couple of options, even if it feels like you are in a living nightmare.

The most natural reaction is to be upset about what happened. But after this reaction, there is a dark rabbit hole that you'll want to avoid. Let's look at your options below.

First thought: "This was the absolute worst time for this to happen."
Second thought: "It is a definite bummer. I'm going to research how the best athletes handle injuries like this."

First thought: "My entire year is ruined."
Second thought: "I'm going to use this time as an opportunity, and I'll get back sooner than I think."

First thought: "What if I never get back to my same level?"
Second thought: "I'm going to be even better when I come back."

First thought: "The next few months are going to be a total waste."
Second thought: "I'm going to use this time to balance my life, strengthen my mind, and focus even more on academics."

As you see, you can choose which thoughts will lift you up and which will end up hurting you. Of course, getting injured is very disappointing, especially if it's going to take you out for a long time—maybe even the whole season. Even if it's a mild injury, allow yourself a moment to have these negative thoughts and feelings. It is normal to be down about what happened. Referencing the first and second thoughts on the previous page might help as you begin to accept the reality of the injury.

But then, sooner than later, you will want to find a different perspective—one that turns this situation into an opportunity. It can be a chance to strengthen your mental toughness and increase your feelings of gratitude for the sport you love. With this mindset, you will be shocked at how much better you feel once you return. You will also appreciate the day-to-day climb back, which will be tedious at times, between rehab and appointments, but it will all have more meaning for you with this mindset. It will make all the difference.

I was talking to an athlete recently who fractured his toe. He told me, "I like seeing this situation as almost a requirement for me to pass to the next level. It's keeping me sort of okay with things, and I am pretty optimistic that I can do what I need to do and not feel complete misery, you know?"

You also now have more time to devote to getting stronger. If you injured your lower body, get to work on your upper body, and vice versa. You could seriously move the needle and build up strength in areas that you haven't had the time to devote to previously.

After a devastating leg injury in May 2011, Buster Posey, World Series champion and former San Francisco Giants catcher known for his calm leadership and clutch performances, returned the next spring healed and even more mentally tough than before. He powered through the Giants' 2012 postseason with grit—capping a tied Game 5 with a bases-loaded grand slam to avoid elimination—and later caught Matt Cain's perfect game, admitting even he was as nervous as he'd ever been. Yet in that moment, his focus never wavered.

Buster Posey was determined to become even better than he was before the injury, and he proved it.

After yet another serious leg injury, Tiger Woods, former number one golfer and five-time Masters champion, after being asked about how scared he felt after another leg injury, admitted, "It wasn't as scary as you might think. I came out saying, 'You mean I'm going to have all of my limbs and maybe even run?' I said, 'Really?'" Tiger was grateful to be able to walk. That's true perspective.

Then, he went on to adjust his swing and began to hit even harder than before, which led to a tournament win, despite a major car accident that could have paralyzed him.

There will be many things that happen in your life—some positive and some that will be disappointing. The hardest part is accepting the things that you didn't expect to happen, circumstances that get in your way of achieving your goals, or events that conflict with the expectations you may have had. We can get stuck wishing secretly to ourselves that things were different, and replay this constantly in our minds. The sooner you catch yourself in this loop and shift your mindset, the better you will feel and the more you will benefit from the extra time to strengthen both your mind and body.

If nothing else, remember this prayer (called the Serenity Prayer): "God, grant us the serenity to accept the things we cannot change, the courage to change the things we can, and the wisdom to know the difference." You will be back. Keep the faith and build your mind one day at a time.

The Mental Road Map of Recovery

1. Accept the reality of what happened. It's okay to be upset. It happened. Now what?

2. Decide to optimize the time away from your sport. You can use it to become mentally and physically stronger.

3. Believe in a full recovery. Positive thoughts will speed up your healing time.

4. Take pride in the incremental progress day-to-day.

5. Practice being present in the moment throughout the day, from task to task, to improve your focus and increase your overall satisfaction.

You get to choose your attitude in any circumstance. How you approach an injury is another opportunity to become mentally stronger.

SECTION 6

Resilience & Adaptability

SETBACKS ARE GUARANTEED. WHAT you do with them isn't.

In this section, you'll learn how to turn failure, frustration, and uncertainty into fuel for growth. Resilience is about staying in the game—mentally and emotionally—even when the path forward isn't smooth.

From injuries to transitions to personal doubts, these chapters will help you respond to adversity with strength, creativity, and purpose. Resilient athletes aren't unshaken—they're resourceful

In this section, you'll learn how to:

- Reframe setbacks as part of the process.
- Embrace discomfort as a training ground.
- Persist when things don't go as planned.

26

Trust the Recruitment Process

How many times have you been asked the question, "So, are you going to play in college?" Whether you've just started getting serious about your sport or you're in the phase of choosing schools, talking to coaches, and visiting campuses, this goal can become stressful very fast.

Even if you aren't yet in high school, the goal of playing in college can still eat away at your raw enjoyment of the game. You may notice some anxious thoughts creeping in, especially as this decision gets closer.

"What if I don't get accepted into a good school? Am I good enough to play D1? Will I even make the high school or travel lineup this year?"

These high-pressure situations are felt daily by high school athletes across the United States. All your hard work probably feels like it's coming down to a few upcoming events. Is your coach also getting more stressed out lately? You heard that this whole college process thing wasn't easy, but now it's coming toward you. On top of it all, you might be attending a college recruiting camp where numerous coaches will be watching you.

Gulp. You think: *"What if I don't perform well? This could all be for nothing if I don't get into a good college."*

Recently, a baseball player confided in me about his anxiety after he had a few bad games in a row. The pressure of the college recruitment process began to weigh on him. *"This is not the time to be in a slump,"* he thought.

Even though the idea of slumps is a negative, self-defeating label that tends to keep you unnecessarily stuck in the problem, I challenged him anyway and asked, "What if you are in a slump?"

"Well," he replied, "I'll probably be benched. And then I'd lose my chance to show coaches what I can do."

"What if that happens?" I pressed further, wanting to see how far he might go with this line of thinking.

He paused and looked a little surprised by my question as if to say, *"Isn't being benched bad enough?"* But he continued, "Well, then I won't get into a good college."

I could see how deep this athlete was in the hole, so I asked, "Well, what if you don't get into a good college?"

"Well, I probably won't get a good job," he replied matter-of-factly.

I hung in there with him. "Okay. What if you don't land a really good job?"

Without hesitation, he replied, "I'll probably end up homeless."

His fear of being homeless might sound extreme, but that's how fear operates. It can be hard to turn it off once it turns into this kind of brushfire. Without awareness and a shift in perspective, college recruiting can trigger this type of fear and send you spiraling.

Perhaps you, too, are surprised by the intensity of your feelings as you face this anxiety. Once again, as we discussed earlier in Chapter 16, "Create a New Relationship with Your Nerves," we don't typically do well with uncertainty. And this is the most uncertain time imaginable for you—a worry that is starting to show up earlier for athletes in their athletic journey.

I can imagine that when you set your sights on playing your sport in college at twelve years old, you had no idea how big this would grow in your mind. At some point, maybe you imagined a coach calling you to tell you how excited she is to have you join their program. Or maybe you could picture finally pulling that letter out of the mailbox one day, stamped ACCEPTED.

Both scenarios are certainly possible. It's just getting through this year, or the next few months, that seems daunting. First, this process will go much more smoothly if you first accept that stress in this situation is normal. Just for a moment, let's consider applying the principle of gratitude that you have this "problem." I know this is a stretch right now. But you do get a choice.

Remember that only 6.5 percent of athletes in the US are even recruited to play in college. If this is your plan, you are among the elite.

So, how can you manage this added pressure and not feel too discouraged when a college coach shows interest but then suddenly disappears? First, right now, give yourself some props for coming this far. It is a big accomplishment. Recognize that you've worked hard over the years, and in many ways, you're exactly where you've always wanted to be. Don't let the natural increase in stress surprise you. You care about your future school and want to make a good choice to capitalize on all your hard work—these are completely rational thoughts.

However, here is what I encourage you to do instead to get through this difficult time: Acknowledge that, as challenging as this phase is, it will pass. Life is inherently uncertain, and this is another opportunity to flex your mental toughness. Just like you are learning to do when you feel some adrenaline or tension in competition, you accept what you can control and let go of what you don't. You cannot fully control the coaches' choices or the outcome.

But you choose to believe that it will work out—that you will end up at the right school for you. It may or may not be the one you initially envisioned in your mind, but things have a way of working out.

Ultimately, if you don't like your choice, remember that it's one of those decisions that can be changed. I'm not suggesting you plan to transfer, but thousands of athletes do this every year. Personally, I started at Auburn University as a freshman. The coach recruited me, and while I had a great time and improved, I realized after a year that I preferred the beach and ocean, a balanced life, and a more competitive tennis schedule. The practices at Auburn weren't intense enough, and I had a distant idea that I might want to play professionally. So, I transferred to an amazing school, UC Santa Barbara, where I continued to improve, lived near the beach, and had a fantastic college experience. It worked out perfectly, even though my first choice wasn't ideal.

This is how we learn in life: by making choices. Some work out right away, while others don't. But they often lead to new opportunities *because* of that initial choice. When they don't, we adapt. You don't need to view the college decision as life and death. I'm here to tell you that there is a school out there for you, even if it's not the exact one you had your heart set on.

Stay open and trust the process. In the meantime, prioritize some principles and strategies from this book, re-engage with a mastery mindset, and focus on what you can control. This approach is your best option and will help you get through this challenging maze.

Continue to build your game. Find joy in your small daily accomplishments, even if they don't seem significant enough in the moment. It all adds up. Prioritize your mindset. When you do this, you'll discover that you can play with less stress and renewed freedom, despite this very challenging time in your life. Let this outcome unfold as you trust yourself and the process.

27

Embrace Discomfort

I'M SURE YOU KNOW what it feels like to be firing on all cylinders, when everything is clicking and it feels effortless. You anticipate the best move without even thinking about it. These rare days feel amazing, don't they?

If only every day could be like that. But they're not—for anyone—not even for the very best athletes in your sport. However, this is where the opportunity lies for you—the fork in the road that separates the best from the rest. You will find the answer in your willingness to embrace the discomfort and to tolerate the stress without letting it take you down.

As Payton Manning said, "Pressure is something you feel when you don't know what the hell you are doing."

Certainly, you know moments like this—when you don't know what to do next. In one moment, you're performing at a high level, and suddenly, after even a single mistake, you find yourself just trying to mentally hang on. Within minutes, maybe seconds, you are left wondering whether you can get your game back, whether you even still have a chance to win.

A successful golfer I was working with had a horrible loss immediately following his best results as a pro. He told me that he let a recent round slip away in a tournament because he felt so horrified by his performance. He didn't even want to discuss it with me, worried it might make it worse to talk about it and bring it out in the open.

"I didn't want to give too much attention to that performance," he told me. "I worry it might make me overthink things even more. I already think too much, you know? But I'm probably overthinking this, too. I just remember playing so badly that I couldn't stop thinking, 'How will I ever make it on the pro tour if my level can drop this low?'"

"Yeah, I understand," I said. "It's really frustrating when you don't play at the level you know you can."

But then I saw a light bulb go on. He continued, "I just realized I was punishing myself for playing so badly, and I'm pretty sure I purposely gave up because of it. I couldn't stand the feeling of playing like that."

"Yeah," I agreed. "It sounds like you self-destructed because you didn't want to experience those feelings. It felt too uncomfortable, and you wanted to avoid it. It's understandable."

However, it is here that the road of mastery will keep you on the right path with guardrails so you can embrace these stressful moments without hitting the eject button.

A gymnast came to me after a painful loss and told me, "My coach tells me that it's good to sit with my feelings, but I'm not sure that will help. Just telling yourself it's okay to feel bad doesn't seem right."

The truth is, feeling uncomfortable is exactly what you need to get better. Embracing discomfort—whether it's discussing your feelings with your coach or parents, taking shots when you lose a little belief, or being more vocal with your teammates, especially when you don't want to—can fast-track your improvement.

When I was a pro and in college, my best training blocks and results happened after I felt the sting of a loss, especially after a really disappointing one. It's ironic: The more we give ourselves permission to feel, the more we can accept the stress and discomfort that shows up. Embracing these moments will help you become a more courageous athlete.

Think about it: You lift weights at the gym, stressing your muscles until they become sore. You do this to get stronger, even though it doesn't always feel good. You're willing to endure this pain because you know it will help you. The same idea applies to your emotions and mental toughness. When you accept the sting of costly mistakes and frustrating losses, you will move forward even faster—taking in the lessons and not getting stuck in your head. We're taught to be "tough" and maintain a positive attitude, but this can only happen when we are honest with ourselves and confront our feelings head-on.

Of course, we all want to feel "good" as often as we can—confident, secure, successful, excited—rather than "bad"—filled with shame, disappointment, fear, and stress. However, this isn't realistic. To grow, you need to allow yourself to feel uncomfortable, even embrace it, which you have already proven you can do. I know this because you are still here.

Now, everything is possible for you—if you approach it with a mastery mindset. You are on your way. I believe in you.

A Guided Visualization: Dropping into the Mastery Mindset Before Competition

THIS GUIDED VISUALIZATION IS for any athlete, playing any sport, to help reset, focus, and compete with a mastery mindset. You can also listen to me personally guide you with this visualization in my audiobook.

Please close your eyes and begin taking slow, deep breaths in through your nose . . . and out through your mouth.

This is your opportunity to let go.

Let your mind settle.

Let your body begin to relax.

Start to gently bring your attention to your breath—the air entering your body through your nose . . . and flowing out through your mouth.

Take deep, calming breaths all the way down into your stomach—filling it up like a balloon.

Feel your abdomen expand as you breathe in . . . and soften as you breathe out.

Don't worry if your thoughts wander. Just notice them—
and let them pass like leaves floating down a river.

You are not your thoughts. You are the one observing.

Now feel your body begin to release tension.

Let it drain down from your forehead . . .

Down through your jaw and shoulders . . .

Flowing like a waterfall down your arms and legs.

Total relaxation.

Letting go. Letting go.

Now imagine you're arriving at a place you know well—a
field, a court, a track, a gym—wherever you train and compete.
See the environment clearly. The sights. The sounds. The smell
of the air.

You feel calm, ready, and grounded. This is where you
belong.

You begin warming up—feeling the rhythm in your body,
the ground beneath your feet.

Your movements are smooth and intentional.

You are connected to your body—alert, relaxed, and
focused.

There's no pressure, no judgment. Just presence.

Your eyes are sharp. Your breath is steady.

You're aware of how your body moves, how it flows.

You listen to your movements—the sound of your footwork, the ball, your breath.

This is what it feels like to be fully locked in.

Now picture yourself stepping into competition.

You take a deep breath and center yourself.

You are calm. Focused. Ready.

You feel strong and capable—not because you're trying
harder, but because you've let go of what doesn't serve you.

You're performing freely now.

No fear. No overthinking.

You trust your body. You trust your training.

You're not trying to be perfect—you're just fully here, moment to moment.

You feel alive in the challenge.

You're competing on your terms, playing with purpose and composure—no matter the score.

You're in control of your mind.

You know how to reset.

You know how to refocus.

And when distractions arise, you simply shift your attention back to your breath, your body, your next move.

This is what you've been training for—not just the skills, but the state of mind.

You are becoming the athlete you imagined.

Loose. Focused. Confident.

Not because everything is easy—but because you've learned how to handle it.

This is what mastery feels like.

Now, I'm going to count back from 5 to 1.

When I reach 1, you'll open your eyes—calm, refreshed, and confident in your body and mind.

5 – You are calm and loose

4 – Your mind is focused

3 – More present in your body

2 – Feel your toes, move your fingers

1 – Open your eyes—refreshed, grounded, and ready

Use this the night before your event or twenty to thirty minutes before you compete to drop into your ideal performance state.

Afterword

DID MY EFFORT TO finish this book pay off for you? Did I keep your attention long enough for you to absorb some of these principles and the tools that go with them? I hope so. I know there is a lot of noise out there, but if you commit to applying the mastery mindset, I promise you will be rewarded.

Whether you read the entire book or just one chapter, at the very least, you now understand that you have options when stress and pressure strike.

Deep mental toughness doesn't happen overnight. But you may find that some of these tools and principles are helpful immediately. Certain principles may work better now, and others will be more helpful down the road.

The key is that you are now on the path of self-mastery. If you want the best outcomes, as I know you do, along with the satisfaction that comes with this success, there is no better path to take.

Certainly, for the next five to ten years—and probably your entire life—the world is going to try to tell you what you should do and how you should think. Remember my view on the word "should" in Chapter 3.

Of course, some of the teachings you receive from coaches, teachers, and parents will be very helpful. My hope is that you can also occasionally stop and ask yourself, *"What do I feel about that?"* or *"What do I want to do?"*

Just because other people focus excessively on their place on the team, rankings, or status, it doesn't mean you have to think the same way. You are your own person.

You know what? There will never be anyone exactly like you in the rest of human history. Remember this. Form your own opinions, be curious, ask for feedback, but ultimately know that your choices and execution of these choices are yours to make.

I encourage you to write down your top two tools or strategies in this book and consistently chip away at them in practice and during competition. Block out time—even just ten minutes in every practice—to focus on one of these tools exclusively. Then, go on to the next.

Before practice or competition, set clear intentions—and make them a priority. Afterward, take a few minutes to reflect and journal about how it went. This helps strengthen your mental habits over time.

Remember: You're better than you think. When that inner voice gets loud during competition, you now understand that it is often inaccurate and unhelpful. If it's not lifting you up, helping you focus, or keeping you in the fight—send it on a vacation to Hawaii. Seriously. It means well, but sometimes it's still stuck in survival mode, reacting to old fears. Your job now is to upgrade it—to help it stay grounded in the present and support you in real time, not drag you into the past or future.

You now have a fully installed remote control for your mind. Your job is to figure out which buttons help you reset and refocus—and use them when it counts.

I wish you success and deep fulfillment as you walk with intention through your journey of mastery. This path is a gift you give yourself. One day, when you look back on your life and think about your competitive experience, you won't need to imagine what could have been. You will know you took ownership of your choices, had the courage to step up under pressure—and that made all the difference.

The Mental Edge Parent's Guide for Young Athletes

Introduction

IT WAS LATE SUMMER, just before school started, and I was at the local pool watching my six-year-old daughter glide through the water with bated breath. She wasn't the front-runner, but she certainly wasn't dead last, either. Across the pool, I spotted her mother, who also seemed to be struggling to catch her breath as she cheered our daughter on. When she was just three, we had a hunch we'd be spending many sunny weekends at an indoor pool. From an early age, she swam like a dolphin; she loved it. But now, at six years old and in her first race, I couldn't believe my eyes. After one lap, it was official—my daughter was in last place.

As the initial shock morphed into mild anxiety, I felt a hint of disappointment. Then came the guilt and shame for actually caring so much—not necessarily about her winning but about her feeling embarrassed.

Sometimes it's hard to tell where our hope for our kids to enjoy competing ends and our desire for them to win begins. But after all, she was just six years old, and this was her very first race. In retrospect, it may have been too early for her to compete. Or maybe it was too early for me.

As I made my way over to my wife to commiserate, I was briefly interrupted by the father of one of my daughter's close friends, who excitedly asked the universally loaded question, "So, how did she do?"

Irritated, I snapped back, "She had fun."

His daughter had come in first place, and he didn't hesitate to share that detail with me. When I finally reached my wife, who was standing by the pool and toweling off our daughter, I whispered, "How are you doing?" She responded with a forced smile, "I'm having some feelings right now." In that moment, I instantly understood what she meant—we were becoming newly indoctrinated victims of the modern sports culture.

Here's the irony: I'm a sports and performance psychology consultant and family therapist who helps athletes, coaches, and parents manage these situations every day. If you put me in my office and presented this exact scenario, I would have said something like, "I know how hard this can be. If you can keep perspective relative to the outcome and emphasize her effort instead, that will help a lot. Talk about what she learned and the enjoyment she had. The results will follow."

That's sound advice. But let's face it—when your child is on the chopping block, it's anything but easy to manage your own inner tornado, depending on how things are going.

You may also have a few questions about how to handle these situations that are bound to come up constantly. Raising a child in competitive sports can be an emotional roller coaster.

You're wise to find a path that helps reduce the ups and downs, and think about some of these questions that many parents have:

- Why does my child perform beautifully in practice but is a different athlete in competition?
- What can I do to help my child feel less anxious and frustrated?
- Do you have any suggestions on how to help my child stop obsessing over results and rankings?
- What can I do when my child is in a slump and losing motivation?
- What should I say to them when they lose?

Over 70 percent of youth athletes quit their sport by age sixteen because they no longer enjoy the experience. The likelihood of your child becoming a scholarship athlete after high school is around 15 percent, and the chance of making it to the pros is only 2 percent of that number. With this in mind, helping your child develop a mastery mindset will not only aid their success but also increase the likelihood that they'll enjoy the incredible benefits sports can offer, even if they don't become a professional. This mindset shift is the most significant win of all. Wherever you find yourself on this athletic roller coaster as a parent, I understand the challenge.

Staying calm and seeing the big picture in the moment is definitely the right approach. However, that's a rational response, and rational judgment often fails us in the heat of the moment, especially when it comes to our children. As parents, we want our children to excel, grow, and be happy.

The reality is that we will make mistakes along the way, but we can learn from them, in the same way we're asking our kids to learn from their mistakes. By doing so, we can help our children compete and, simultaneously, develop into healthy individuals along the way.

This guide is designed to help you navigate the common—and often inevitable—challenges of parenting an athlete with practical, real-world strategies. The tools you'll explore here complement the mindset, principles, and exercises your child is learning throughout this book and the *Mental Edge Workbook*, if you're using both.

This section will also help you build your own coping skills, so you can more confidently support your child's growth, both on and off the field. These parenting tools are key to raising well-rounded, resilient kids as they pursue success through the path of mastery.

1

Put Yourself in Their Shoes

WHEN I WAS A young athlete, losing a tennis match or a baseball game felt devastating. It tore my heart apart. I vividly remember climbing into my mother's car after a loss, feeling as though the world had come to an end. It truly felt that bad. In my young mind, accepting the reality of the loss wasn't even an option.

A child's young brain sees the world in black and white, with hardly any gray area. So, whether they've just experienced a soul-crushing defeat or are gearing up to compete in a few hours, their emotions are running high. They don't yet have an air traffic controller in their brain to help manage this inner chaos.

When they lose, they want the whole experience to disappear. When nerves hit before an event, they simply want reassurance that they will perform well and win—neither of which may happen. This is the beauty of sports; competition teaches kids so many invaluable life lessons.

It's essential to remember that after a loss, kids desperately wish they could turn back time and alter the outcome. They are often in disbelief, extremely disappointed, and angry.

As a parent of a young athlete, you know it takes a little time before they can calm down. It's helpful to give them some space to process the loss for themselves without outside input. The first thirty minutes after an event are usually too hot to touch—and rarely productive—especially after they lose. If you can avoid throwing fuel onto the fire, they will soon realize there is nothing they can do to change it.

This is where you come in. You need to act as their emotional air traffic controller until they learn how to soothe themselves. These parenting moments can become some of their greatest gifts if you can remain calm, which may be your toughest challenge, too, despite being a fully developed adult. We all get triggered from time to time, and competition with outcomes that involve our kids will test us to no end.

The magic lies in how you respond in these high-emotional moments. What do you say when your child says, "I hate this sport. I want to quit"?

Even though your child's reaction may instill panic in you as she looks down, sulking, and says, "That was the worst game ever," this is the moment of truth—a chance that will undoubtedly arise countless times before she heads off to college. The temptation to rush in and either talk her out of her negative mindset or critique her performance can be overpowering. Every parent knows this moment.

Sadly—and I've fallen into this trap plenty of times—most of us approach it from one of two angles: trying to wrestle our child out of their difficult feelings or offering tips on how to improve next time.

In these gut-wrenching moments, I encourage you to put on your oxygen mask, take a deep breath, and remember that this is part of their learning and development. Perhaps you can shift your perspective and focus on feeling grateful that your child cares about something this much instead of them sitting in front of the TV or playing video games. Despite the pain of losing, you remember, they are exercising, growing, and building resilience for the future. These are the sweat-equity challenges that you and your child will have a chance to embrace over your remaining years in competitive sports.

This is the moment where empathy—a crucial life skill for all children to learn—can become your greatest asset. Instead of saying, "Well, there are a lot more games to play; you just need to let it go" or "Next time, just be a little more aggressive," try to meet your child where they are. You could say, "I know that stung today, but I loved watching you play, and I'm proud of you for never giving up." (Make sure you are referencing something they actually demonstrated, even if it wasn't throughout the entire event.)

I understand how tempting it is to try to change your child's perspective right away—to help them see that a mistake or loss isn't as terrible as it might feel in the moment. Or, how your desire to correct their mistakes is eating you alive. You are convinced that if they had passed more decisively, taken more open shots, and not gotten so negative, the outcome would have been very different.

Upon reflection, I now understand how paralyzed and desperate my mother felt when I would be in tears over a loss. Like most parents, she struggled with seeing me in such a destructive state of mind and had no idea how to handle my torrent of emotions. Even thirty-five years later, she still gasps at these memories and says, "Oh, Jeff. It was just awful. There was nothing I could have done." To her credit, she did try—in her own desperate way. Believe it or not, my mother would bribe me with a new sweatsuit or a trip to my favorite restaurant if I would calm down. She simply didn't know what to do. I don't blame her.

While nothing can take away the immediate pain of a loss, responding with empathy can be the best first step in helping to relax our kids' nervous systems. At the very least, it can help diminish their need to escalate their emotions in order for you to see how much they're suffering, and it will minimize any potential arguments.

When you see your child emotionally overwhelmed after missing a shot or feeling inconsolable after a gut-wrenching loss to a weaker opponent, we can't fully relate to or accurately remember what their inner experience truly feels like. Telling them how we think they should feel or what they need to do better—based on our perspective—will likely make things worse, leading them to believe you don't understand.

However, if we can pause and approach the situation with empathy, we can imagine how challenging it is for them, given their age and level of competitiveness. If we're asking kids to embrace challenges, accept emotional ups and downs, and stay committed to training, we need to do the same ourselves.

You might say something like, "Just keep working hard; more wins will come. I really enjoyed watching you play, and I'm proud of you." Remember, shorter messages are often more effective with kids.

Please commit this to memory, as it's easy to forget in the moment. Just as I encourage my athletes to internalize key intentions before events, you can develop a post-event emotional management plan, too.

Whether your child is heading toward college or a professional path, your approach to winning and losing should remain consistent: focus on enjoying their play and appreciating their effort. If you can help them view these moments as learning opportunities—absorbing the positive lessons despite the pain—you've done an excellent job.

I understand that things won't always go as smoothly as described; your child might stay stuck in negativity for a while, even with your support. They might sulk off the field and say very little. Kids often cope by shutting down emotionally, which is a common reaction. Just be patient.

Think of this post-event scenario as tending to a garden. Flowers don't bloom right away, but eventually, with the right care, they will flourish. Empathy is the water that helps them grow.

It's tempting to get caught up in the winning and losing mindset, often due to concerns about their self-confidence or your own unresolved feelings about success. These worries are valid.

However, if you focus on your child's progress and effort, allowing the results to become secondary to the broader context of their development—such as nurturing a passion for their sport and a positive connection to exercise—you will be giving your child a lifelong runway that includes health, resiliency, personal satisfaction, and success.

2

Tread Lightly When Offering Advice

Dɪᴅ ʏᴏᴜ ᴇᴠᴇʀ ɢᴇᴛ annoyed when your parents told you what to do as a child? Perhaps you not only felt annoyed but even hated it. But I imagine the step from feeling this and communicating it to your parents was not a small one. Your kids likely feel the same way, unless you happen to have one of those highly intense, sensitive kids who doesn't yet have a filter.

I'm certainly not suggesting you shouldn't guide your child. Of course, kids need guidance. They shouldn't get to make all the choices or always get what they want—not by a long shot.

That said, when it comes to teaching your child, particularly when they hit the middle teen years, I encourage you to build in a pause button—a similar button your kids learned in the first part of this book. It's important to be mindful when coaching our children because what we say and how we say it can affect them well beyond sports. If you say too much—especially when they are upset, shut down, or feeling stressed—you risk losing your invaluable connection to them. This holds true even if you are the primary coach for your child who is playing individual sports.

As a former coach and professional athlete myself, I learned this lesson firsthand. Early on, when I tried to offer my son, Will, some advice about his game, he shot back, "Dad, what do you know?" In fact, after my first attempt to give him some instruction, he simply dropped his racquet and said, "This isn't fun anymore," and walked off the court. I got the message loud and clear. At least, that moment opened my eyes.

It's tough to watch our kids make mistakes, especially when they're nervous, emotional, or playing poorly for no apparent reason. It's natural to want to help them fix something that's getting in their way.

As you become more aware of your interactions with your child—a skill your child is also developing—you'll notice other parents overcoaching from the sidelines. You'll see them yelling, trying to fix whatever their child may be doing wrong. Those who aren't yelling are likely thinking the same thing but have just enough awareness to hold it inside.

Personally, I found it helpful to jot down my thoughts in these moments so I could share them with my son's coach the following week. I recognized this huge rabbit hole early enough to channel my emotions in a productive way—most of the time.

This tendency to over-instruct our kids and talk excessively about the last event can create unnecessary pressure, making the experience less enjoyable for our kids. It may not seem like a big deal at the time, but every sign you give your child that you are invested in their success will be noted. If they begin to think that you care too much, they will begin caring less to balance things out. Trust me, you don't want to find yourself on the wrong side of this ledger if you can avoid it. Every interaction matters.

Sometimes, we offer our child input out of sheer enthusiasm. There are other moments when we have a knee-jerk reaction and yell at them on the field as our own adrenaline starts ramping up. We think that the sooner they understand, the better it will be for them. Unbeknownst to us, we might also be unconsciously projecting our own past hopes and disappointments onto them.

Identifying these deeper motivations can be challenging, especially within ourselves. As devoted parents of young athletes, we naturally harbor competitive urges. I'll admit that while watching my son compete, I've thought, *"A little win today would really boost his confidence and ranking."*

I've also felt pressure to share the lessons from my own tennis career and sports expertise with him. I've even scolded myself, saying, *"Come on, Jeff. You're a sports psychologist. You should be helping him more."* My son, now sixteen, often rolls his eyes and says, "Here comes another life lesson." But I listen to him, I pause, and I usually end up laughing. Sometimes I just didn't realize when I was slipping into the "I-need-to-impart-my-wisdom" mode.

Why do we do this? Out of fear that our kids might struggle—both on the field and off—while under our watch. It's a gulp-worthy thought. It's normal to want to protect our kids and help them succeed. But we need to pay attention to the degree to which we get involved in their day-to-day development. If we overstep, we put our kids and our relationship in jeopardy.

During the first six months of my son's competitive journey, whenever I saw him make mistakes—like not switching his grip or hitting the ball without focus—as I mentioned, I felt an anxious pressure. I worried about potential major technical overhauls down the line, and I wanted to ensure he'd become the best athlete he could be.

Mainly, I wanted to avoid unnecessary stalls in his development. I admit that I would cringe a little internally when he missed shots due to poor technique, which I was convinced he was doing just to drive me crazy. Recognizing his strong reactions, I understood that directly telling him how to fix it wouldn't go over well. So, I stifled my emotions and restrained my urge to fix things. I think he noticed my reactions anyway.

I often felt inadequate—sometimes I still do—when my son wouldn't take my advice, which was most of the time. But I thought, *"Why can't he just take my advice without having it feel as though I don't believe in him?"*

He would accept it on occasion if I mentioned something at the right time and in the right context. But usually he didn't want to hear it from me. This is also normal.

While it's crucial to learn about respect, composure under pressure, and other life skills, directly coaching your child can quickly become a slippery slope. Why? They want you to think they are great and that you believe in them. It's subconscious, even if they act like they don't care. They desperately want your approval. This creates an obvious conflict, doesn't it? Even if they seem like they're listening to your tips and enduring this dynamic, there is a big risk they will begin distancing themselves from you to maintain their autonomy.

Yet, despite this resistance, they are still watching you closely. They are observing and listening to every gesture and word—mostly in search of approval or disapproval. If you struggle to control your emotions and find yourself expressing disappointment, they may begin to tune you out to defend themselves psychologically. This would be a huge loss. Make no mistake, kids are experts at tuning us out. While it may seem like they're listening, all they see is our lips moving.

In my quest for understanding, I've asked several kids—including my own—how it feels when parents yell instructions from the sidelines or talk too much about results. Here's a summary of what they shared:

- "It's really distracting."
- "It's embarrassing."
- "It makes me not want to play."
- "It's not fun anymore."
- "It adds pressure."

Despite these booby traps, it is possible—albeit not always easy—to earn your child's trust and attention with a more balanced, long-term approach. You can still guide and support them while respecting their autonomy and feelings.

It took some creativity and persistence to find this balance with my son. Earlier, I mentioned how he felt when I gave him a few tips, and he proceeded to walk off the court.

Of course, you didn't think I was going to give up that easily? I got him back on the court again, but I definitely felt like I was under a microscope.

Nevertheless, as I let some more time pass, I tried again. Cheerfully, I walked to the net and said, "Buddy, can I share an idea with you?" I kept it general so he wouldn't immediately go on the defensive.

This time, I anticipated a positive response from him—maybe something like, "Okay, sure. What is it?" Unfortunately, life had other plans. Without missing a beat, he scrunched his face and shot back, "No!" before turning and heading back to the baseline. Internally frustrated yet maintaining a smile, I replied, "Okay. No problem." Plan B was officially out the window.

About thirty minutes later, amidst a good rally, I came up with another idea. In my mind, I was thinking that, even though I had no interest in being his coach, at the very least, I wanted to make sure that the time between his lessons wouldn't be a total waste.

So, this time I walked up to the net and excitedly exclaimed, "That was an awesome rally! You're really following through!" I let the compliment sit for a moment before adding, "Just remember to switch the grip on the backhand. Good playing, buddy." To my relief, he nodded with a slight smile and replied, "Okay."

In that moment, I thought to myself, "Holy crap, that was easy! If he can grasp this technical issue now, it might save us thousands of dollars in lessons down the road!" This experience reaffirmed the importance of patience, timing, and the benefits of open communication.

But I have to admit, I felt like I had pulled a fast one on him. He didn't seem to negatively react to the correction I made, and it seemed like he absorbed the tip from me. What I employed was the "sandwich technique"—start with a positive comment, deliver the intended message, and follow up with another positive remark.

Using this method, especially in the right context and with the right timing, can be very effective.

However, it's crucial to be cautious about "dosing"—the balance of information is key. You need to say enough, but not overwhelm them. In other words, less is more here.

Nothing is more repellent to kids than adults repeating themselves, especially if kids perceive they are failing at something. If you notice you're talking too much without getting any response from them, hit the pause button and give them space. If you find yourself doing 90 percent of the talking, it's a sign you're losing them. The good news? It's never too late to shift this dynamic with some honest conversation and a touch of humility.

Sadly, kids today seem to have less patience—especially with parents—and their attention spans are shrinking daily. They can also be highly sensitive to criticism, which makes them more defensive. Had I not identified something positive to mention to my son at the start of that conversation on the court, it's clear he would not have been open to my feedback.

When you share a strong connection with your child and they are naturally more open and curious, and not overly sensitive and intense, employing this "sandwich approach" is extremely effective. It's a delicate balance, but when you start with a positive comment, your chances of connection increase exponentially.

Even though my initial attempt to share an observation with my son failed, I believe that respecting his need for autonomy by asking for permission increased his receptivity. When children feel that their parents are proud of them, they are also generally more open to feedback.

I can candidly tell you that, while I may still have moments when I see my son doing something that will likely not end in a positive outcome, I've mostly managed to sidestep this large rabbit hole of tension, arguing, and mutual frustration.

Finding balance with your child doesn't happen overnight. Instead of focusing on perfection, think in terms of increments and percentages. Just as your child works on being calmer after mistakes, you can develop your own self-awareness when it comes to communicating with them, especially when they are competing.

Achieving balance in this dynamic will yield great rewards over time. Conversely, if you struggle to regulate your emotions in response to your child's sports journey, your words may unintentionally add pressure, risking harm to your overall relationship. Sports provide an incredible opportunity to build a lifelong connection with your children if you pay attention and are willing to grow alongside them.

Next time you feel the urge to impart your hard-earned wisdom, consider the impact and the bigger picture. Use the feedback "sandwich" to enhance your chances of breaking through their natural defensive barriers.

While competitive sports can be a nerve-racking tightrope to walk at times, with the right perspective, it will become one of your most treasured memories.

3

Normalize Their Pre-Event Nerves

PRE-EVENT JITTERS CAN TAKE a toll and ruin the day, creating an emotional roller coaster for the entire family. You notice it when your child grunts at you in the morning, barely finishes half her bagel, or panics when she can't find matching socks. Fun, right?

So, how can you help your child "hijacked" by performance anxiety and unable or unwilling to eat breakfast? You know she'll pay for it later. You think, *"She's going to totally bonk today if she doesn't eat something."* But when you urge her to eat, she replies, "I can't. I feel sick." Sigh.

If you're feeling like pulling your hair out and crawling back into bed, you're not alone. These tense moments are common in homes across the US. Wouldn't it be easier if children would just do what's best for them? Is eating a bagel and hydrating that big of an ask? Oh, the control we wish we had. And how do you handle it when, after another heart-wrenching loss, they declare, "I hate this sport. I want to quit"? You see how well your child performs in practice, only to watch that disappear during a game. They freeze on the soccer field, hesitate to go after the ball, hang their heads, call themselves names, or seem completely disengaged. It's nerve-racking to witness, to say the least.

To give you some context, anxiety among children has been steadily rising over the past few years, skyrocketing recently due to the impact of COVID-19. Previously, about one in three adolescents experienced anxiety, and these numbers only represent reported cases. Post-COVID, those numbers have risen another 25 percent. It has become an epidemic affecting both teenagers and younger children alike.

Understanding Family Anxiety in Kids

Anxiety often runs in families, leaving kids particularly vulnerable to mental health challenges. They struggle with managing their thoughts and feelings, a skill that can be dramatically improved through mental coaching or therapy. At this stage in their lives, their sense of self is weak, but their desire to fit in is strong.

As a result, the uncertainty of competition can be overwhelming. They know their performance will be scrutinized not only during the game, which is nerve-racking enough, but also shared on social media for friends, family, and the world to see. This exposure, coupled with the illusion of perfection often portrayed online, creates an incredibly high level of anxiety. Sports has a way of highlighting these underlying pressures, and while this is an opportunity to develop mental toughness early in their lives, without proper guidance it can also be crippling.

The good news? Many high-profile athletes are now openly discussing their mental health struggles, which has significantly increased awareness among young athletes regarding the importance of developing their mental skills. Athletes of all ages, as well as parents and coaches, are actively seeking expertise in this area. This shift represents major progress, providing young athletes with opportunities to learn valuable life lessons through sports during their formative years.

Now, let's address your child's pre-event jitters and explore your options in these tense moments. As your child nibbles on her bagel, you can simply remind her that pre-game nerves are normal. In fact, you might tell her, "I was reading that Megan Rapinoe used to get nervous before games, too," or share an example of another top athlete in her sport. Then, let it be. Such simple statements can go a long way in these moments. It shows you are attentive and also recognize that nerves are nothing to be ashamed of.

To help manage your own discomfort, it can help to remember that nerves mean that your child cares about what they are doing—they have a passion for something, which is a blessing, even if it is nerve-wracking. But it's also an opportunity to learn how to push through discomfort and develop more self-mastery, which they are learning throughout this book.

For kids, learning to accept these uncomfortable feelings takes time, especially if they've struggled with them for a while. However, when they begin to assert more control over their reactions, their confidence in themselves will grow. Encouraging your children to lean into these feelings—to experience the fear and trust themselves anyway—will pay dividends over time.

It's essential for your child to understand that being nervous is universal—that all athletes must learn to push through this discomfort, knowing that it will fade. As they install the buttons on the remote control I mentioned (kids love this idea) such as diaphragmatic breathing, centering, playing with intention, and shifting their focus to what they control as opposed to what they don't control, they will feel less anxious and more confident, regardless of the adrenaline in their body. We just need to give them space to have their experience while utilizing the tools I've laid out for them in this book.

As you know, young athletes often worry, not only about the outcome of the day, but they also get anxious about being nervous—that's right, anxious that they are anxious. This is the first layer I remove with kids so they can begin to face this universal challenge with more confidence. It's liberating for them when they realize they can learn to embrace this feeling instead of resist it. When this realization occurs, they become more confident, feel in control, and perceive themselves as less of a victim of pre-event tension.

Years ago, a twelve-year-old baseball player, a catcher we'll call Jordan, and his mother sought my help because he was extremely competitive, loathed making mistakes, and would often spiral emotionally during games. His emotional struggles created tension in their relationship, and his pre-game anxiety was overwhelming. After Jordan and his mom filled me in on a few details, she left, and it was just Jordan and me. I prefer starting sessions with younger kids this way to ensure I gather enough context. I remember how his feet barely touched the floor, which struck me then and still does—the way young athletes are forced to face their fears at such tender ages, despite their vulnerability and innocence. This challenge presents a great opportunity when managed mindfully.

However, like many kids I've seen before, Jordan was appropriately skeptical—he doubted that a sports psychologist could simply make all his problems go away.

But for decades, I've observed that when an athlete is motivated to understand what's stopping them from performing up to their ability, positive growth is certain and often relatively swift.

With his mom now gone, we resumed our conversation about Jordan's anxiety. I asked, "So, what does it feel like for you the morning before a game?" My goal was to understand the intensity of his anxiety while building rapport.

"Terrible," he replied. "I feel like I want to throw up."

"It is an awful feeling, isn't it? Hard to eat, too, I bet?"

"Yup," he acknowledged. "I hate it."

"Yeah," I agreed.

"Did you know that pro baseball players feel nervous, too?" He looked interested. "So, how do the nerves hold you back?" I asked.

"I start thinking about striking out and not making good throws," he replied. "I can't help it. Then, I get this horrible feeling in my stomach."

"Do you want to know what the best athletes do when they feel nervous?" I responded.

"Yeah," he said.

"They expect and even accept that this feeling is just a normal part of their warm-up," I explained. "Believe it or not, they even learn to like it."

I could see a light bulb going on in his brain.

You see, when your child sits down to breakfast, if they happen to be struggling with this issue, instead of walking on eggshells and avoiding it, you can simply remind them that nerves are always part of competition. Treat this situation nonchalantly and stay calm, then do your best to keep it light. It's also a good idea to be quiet—especially in the morning with a teenager—and try and steer the conversation to things outside of the event, when possible.

By allowing our children to work through their fears without panicking or overreacting ourselves, they will build more confidence in their ability to manage this very normal experience.

Naturally, young athletes can be quite self-absorbed, believing they are the only ones who feel this way. Initially, they hope the feeling will just vanish. But if they happen to have read the chapter "Create a New Relationship with Your Nerves" earlier in this book, they will also have a new compass to guide them when nerves strike.

Over time, as you reinforce that nerves are just another challenge to be mastered, not something to be feared, you will help your child become mentally tough early in their life.

4

Keep Your Cool When Your Child Loses Theirs

As we discussed earlier, there will be moments when your child's fear of failure and frustration with mistakes escalate into a forest fire. They might bang their racquet, talk back to the refs, be disrespectful to their coach or teammates, or give up, believing there's no chance to win. So, what are your options as a parent?

In these situations, two reactions are likely. One is to ignore it, thinking, "They're nervous, they're competitive, they'll grow out of it; it's not that bad." The other is to yell at them, shame them, and make them feel worse.

Most parents face these emotional moments at some point. Given the pressure to win, kids' developing brains, and their fear of being judged, some negative behavior is inevitable.

This is why it's crucial to be proactive and clarify what matters to you on the competitive sports path—just as I encourage your child to do. Which behaviors are you willing to overlook because you see them as part of the learning process? Just as young athletes need to learn to accept mistakes, you must recognize that your children will, at some point, erupt or lose control.

While it might be tempting to pretend their behavior didn't happen, or to yell at them to make sure they understand the lesson, we can do better. In Chapter 1, I highlighted the power of empathy—acknowledging your child's feelings as a healthy first step.

When they mess up, you might say, "I understand that call by the ref was extremely frustrating. However, what's not okay is how you spoke to him. That doesn't demonstrate mental toughness or leadership for the team. Let's work on keeping your composure next time."

They may very well refute your advice in the moment or ignore it because they're upset and developmentally programmed to react emotionally, but this is where I suggest you hold your ground. If your child says, "Yeah, but that call was a joke! We would have won if he made the right call," you can respond, "Yes, you may be right. I get it; it was super frustrating. But remember, bad calls are part of the game—they will happen again. Let's focus on what you can control, okay?" Your compassionate response will plant a seed for future reflection.

Roger Federer serves as a great example of a player who learned to maintain his composure even when things didn't go his way. However, he wasn't always like this; he could be a poor sport on his "off" days. At fifteen, his parents decided to keep him out of tournaments until he learned to control his emotions, which forced him to quickly develop this vital skill. It can be a tough choice because we don't like it when our kids miss out on competitive opportunities, but it's often a short-term loss for a significant long-term gain. Team sports can be trickier, but you can still reinforce this by collaborating with the coach.

Another effective approach when your child continues to misbehave is to ask them questions that encourage independent thinking. This shifts the conversation to a more collaborative tone. For example, you might prompt them with, "What would be a better response in that situation in the future? What other options can you think of if the ref makes a bad call?"

———————

If they don't engage with you in the moment and seem to shut down or tune you out, simply remind them that maintaining composure is important to you. Express your hope—and even expectation—that they will learn from this experience.

As you can imagine, when your child believes that you care more about their attitude and character than about winning, they will internalize this and positively shift their behavior and mindset—provided the relationship is healthy. However, there's a caveat: If you communicate that attitude matters most while being more invested in their success, they will see right through it.

I understand how challenging it can be to manage emotions in the moment and find the right words when stressed. Sometimes, it may be necessary to set firmer boundaries, such as not allowing them to participate in the next game or tournament if they don't comply or if your values and lessons are clearly not sinking in.

Simply put, without clear values and consistent communication, your child may come to believe that winning is the only thing that matters. This belief can lead to increased anxiety, a drop in performance, and a challenging environment for everyone involved.

Ultimately, we aim to teach our kids resilience, the ability to face challenges, adherence to rules, and persistence. We also want them to think for themselves and reflect on their actions.

In the future, when the games are over and trophies are gathering dust, these parenting decisions may prove to be the most valuable gifts you can give them. By prioritizing their development as human beings, you're choosing to take the long view.

5

Talk About Skill Development, Not Potential

IN THE MINDS OF virtually every young athlete I've worked with over the past twenty-five years, the word "potential" has become a ticking time bomb. For years, I have seen athletes shrink in fear as we discuss their recent performances, recounting the dozens of times their coaches would tell them how much potential they had.

I recall one session in particular with a track and field athlete who couldn't stop worrying about the expectations she was feeling—her own expectations, expectations from her parents, and the worry about disappointing her coach. She admitted that the pressure to win was extremely distracting, even debilitating at times. Now, it was the added worry of getting recruited by a college.

After the session was over, we walked out of the office together and her father immediately asked, "How did it go?"

"It went well," I acknowledged.

However, I had a feeling he might not be satisfied with my response.

Her father continued, "If only she could play like she does in practice, he said. She'd be starting every game. She has so much potential."

I could see his daughter's face turn bright red as she looked down, clearly embarrassed and even more stressed.

"Let's work together to keep this fun and engaging for her, and I'm confident things will improve," I assured him.

As the young girl and her father left my office, he added, "Well, maybe we'll have something 'good' to report after the tournament this weekend."

I understand. It's one of the hardest things we have to deal with as parents—watching our children perform below what we believe they are capable of, let alone watching them blow up emotionally at the drop of a hat.

As a sports parent, this is a constant battle. You may recognize your own tendency to get pulled into this cyclone of anxiety with your child. This increasing pressure for our kids to secure a spot at a reputable university has become an understandable, but also obsessive, quest for many families.

Let me share one more example of a trap that we are all vulnerable to, and that is largely out of many parents' awareness.

As I greeted the parent of one of my athletes on the sidelines of a local lacrosse tournament, I saw him muttering to himself, "Oh, man. She looks really stiff. When she makes mistakes like that, I know she's distracted."

I was curious to know what else he was thinking. He continued. "She always misses that shot. She had all the time in the world. This is going to really mess with her head."

I've witnessed this kind of self-talk countless times—sometimes subtle, sometimes not. I've had thoughts like this, too, at times, even if I didn't verbalize them.

You know exactly what I'm talking about. We are human. Please give yourself a break for a moment. Then, let's get to work on shifting this, slowly but surely.

For starters, even when we think about our child's potential—the gap between where their skills are now and where we believe they should be—let's find an alternative way to help them. The concept of potential for your child will only tighten the handcuffs they feel. It might seem motivating for them to hear this, but it usually isn't. It actually increases their fear of failure. Potential becomes elusive, and there is no "there" in their mind. This idea becomes unattainable to them.

When we communicate this concept directly to our kids, it's a seed that gets firmly planted, especially when repeated. If they don't perform well or meet their own expectations on a given day, the word "potential" will turn toxic. It becomes a crippling burden rather than a source of inspiration.

Here's my suggestion. Focus on the things your kids have full control over—working hard, bouncing back from mistakes, and having the courage to get back on the horse after a tough game.

Replace your judgment and frustration about their progress or the outcome by remaining curious about your child's experience. Rather than fixating on the short-term outcome, ask your child what they learned or what part of the game they felt good about—especially when they tell you it was all "bad."

Use open-ended questions like, "Tell me about the best part of the competition today from your perspective. Did you discover any adjustments that helped you be more aggressive? What did the coach emphasize with the team?"

Also, given the numerous events you will attend over the years, taking time to expand your conversations—whether within sports or on unrelated topics—will create a more relaxed atmosphere for the entire family over time.

This commitment to engage in the things your kids have control over— which will also help them perform better—will alleviate the pressure they feel. It will help them worry less. They will enjoy sports more.

All athletes need to learn that it's not only okay to lose and perform poorly, but that setbacks are vital building blocks for improvement and even greatness.

Again, I understand that witnessing your child's self-incrimination after mistakes can be frustrating and painful, especially when they are being so perfectionistic. It's particularly tough because you know if your child could see that one error doesn't need to define their day, they would play more freely, and enjoy their experience so much more. Your greatest weapon during these recurring moments is to put on your own oxygen mask and recognize how quickly you become emotionally invested in your child's errors and reactions. If we want our children to let go of their errors, we need to be able to do this, too. There are few things more triggering in life than watching our children face a test, game, argument, or any form of danger. These situations can emotionally hijack us, just as they do our kids.

Here are a few tips to summarize some best practices so you can become a more grounded sports parent and give your children the greatest gift of their lifetime:

1. **Be specific with feedback.** When giving feedback, be clear about what you want your child to understand about themselves or their game. Instead of saying, "You're so much better than those girls. Look how well you play in practice," try, "When you attacked the ball like you did today, it really paid off." You might also say, "I loved watching you and the team play." That lets them know your enjoyment is also not tied to their performance. They are just sensitive creatures. You don't need to be perfect, just become more aware of the impact of your words.

2. **Ensure your assessment is genuine.** When discussing your child's abilities, consider all aspects of their development. Be sincere with your feedback; if you don't genuinely believe what you're saying, they likely won't either.

3. **Consider your timing.** To build your child's confidence, provide positive feedback after a victory. This will make them more available to talk about the game and not feel so threatened. Similarly, give them at least thirty minutes of space after they lose to calm down before you engage in any conversation about the event and their experience. If you wait for them to bring it up, that's even better! They are just waiting to hear what they did wrong, especially after a loss. Take as many deep breaths as you need to keep yourself sane.

4. **Focus on learning.** When athletes return from practice or competition and express disappointment about a loss,

keep the focus on the process. After empathizing, ask about what worked and what didn't. If they're willing to talk—which can be rare, so patience is essential—use open-ended questions to foster self-awareness. Avoid sweeping judgments and refrain from comparisons with other teams or athletes, especially siblings! By replacing the word "potential" with "progress," you will spare both you and your child from unnecessary heartache.

5. **Give your child permission to miss.** Your child will appreciate it when you don't highlight their mistakes, especially in the car after a game. Broaden your perspective to embrace all the life lessons your child is gaining through sports. By remaining calm and granting your child permission to miss—whether on the sidelines, in the car after a game, or at the dinner table at home—you'll empower them to do the same.

Make no mistake, the choices you make within the pressure cooker of competitive youth sports will have a long-lasting impact on your child.

As a parent or coach, you are in a unique position to help your child build an alternative, internal "metric" that will lead to the unconditional confidence I discussed in Chapter 9. This kind of lasting confidence, measured against their own capabilities and qualities they can influence, will be a gift that pays dividends over time.

It's important to remember that young athletes' brains are still forming and they will not be fully developed until their late twenties. Therefore, the words you choose and the aspects of competition that you focus on will impact them throughout their entire lives on and off the field. No pressure! Obviously,

I don't intend to frighten you—most kids learn to be resilient sooner or later—but you can help contribute to this crucial skill early in their lives.

With a mindset of mastery in the family and the commitment to follow the principles laid out here, you will ensure that even the most challenging moments will become some of the greatest memories of your lifetime.

Thank You for Reading

I TRULY HOPE *The Mental Edge for Young Athletes* gave you tools and inspiration you can use right away.

If you found value in these pages, would you take just two minutes to leave a short review on Amazon?

Your feedback helps other athletes, parents, and coaches discover the book—and it means the world to me.

Simply go to Amazon, find the book's page, and click "Write a Customer Review." Thank you for your support, and for being part of this mission to help athletes everywhere build their Mental Edge.

With gratitude,
Jeff Greenwald

Acknowledgments

THIS BOOK WOULDN'T EXIST without the many incredible people who've touched my life:

Brent Abel	D.J. Caruso
Kerstin Anderson	James Clear
Chad Andrews	Joel & Marion Cohen
Jimmy Arias	Paul Cohen
ATP Tour	Hugo Colpart
John Austin	Brian Cory
Richard Behar	Jose Cubillos
Nancy Berger	Melinda Czink
Martin Blackman	Pablo Pires De Almeida
Nick Bollettieri	Brett Dickinson
Jonathan Borsuk	Joel Drucker
Laura Bradley	Cliff Drysdale
Kip Brady	Craig Ellison
Chip Brooks	Roy Emerson
Wayne Bryan	Gordie Ernst
Brookes Byrd	Rich & Kathy Fettke
Tom Carey	Craig Flax

Susan Foote

Camilla Georgi

Brad Gilbert

Dan Goldberg

Dean Goldfine

Alejandro Gonzalez

Laurie Goodfellow

Gary Goodman

Len Gordon

Dick Gould

Ally Greenwald

Becca Greenwald

Brendan & Tasha Greenwald

Evan Greenwald

Gabe & Kristen Greenwald

Howard Greenwald

Jake Greenwald

Jamie Greenwald

Kacey Greenwald

Kelly Greenwald

Lexi Greenwald

Marilynn Greenwald

Tyler Greenwald

Will Greenwald

Ren Greenwald

Zach Greenwald

Bill Grimes

Spencer Grimes

Coach Grums

Tim Gullikson

Tom Gullikson

Gimhani Gunasinghe

Birthe Haase

Will Hamilton

Michael Hatfield

Andrew Hawley

Rod Heckelman

Jeff Heely

Jose Hilla

Brooks Hoehn

Charles Hoeveler

Charlie Hoeveler

Matt Holt

HRT

Cal Hunter

ITF

Steve Jackson

Mick Jacobs

Sandy & Marilyn Jones

Pete Karlan

Donna Mae Karnes

William J. Kellogg

Audrey Klein

Matt Knauer

Brad Koontz

Mark Kovacs

Kathy Krickstein

Marc Kriessman

Ulrike Kuehl

Duane Kuiper

Doug Kyle

Patrick Kypson

Shibu Lal
Ricky Landry
Andrea Lawrence
Jim Loehr
Tom Lonergan
Conan Lorenzo
Paul Lubbers
Ginny Stone Mackin
Tim Mahaffy
Marin FC Soccer
Stan Matthews
Chrissy McCambridge
James McLean
Greg Moran
Julio Moros
Scott Morse
Larry Mousouris
Carolina Murphy
Steve Myers
NCTA
Craig Nelson
Kristal Nelson
Pam Nelson
Maia Newman
Nancy Novak
Jay & Donna O'Donnell
Sheila Ohlson
Nate Oppenheim
Karen Orsey
Craig O'Shannessy
Milton Ossorio

Alicia Paulson
Dave Perron
Sean Peterson
Vessa Ponka
Barry Pulliam
Jack Pulliam
Jensen Reiter
Clay Risher
Tracy Rittner
Cezar Robelo
Kristin Rosenbloom
Madeline Rosenbloom
Lisa Rourke
Bill Ruel
Chris Russell
Jeff Salzenstein
Erin Schneider
The Settles Family
Peter Shaper
Justin Sherman
Steve Siegel
Gene Siegel
P.J. Simmons
Stein & Karmin Skaar
Karin Slezak
Scott Slobin
David Smith
Jonathan Smolowe
Elizabeth "Lizzie" Spencer
Jonathan Stokke
Pete Stovell

Erin Tadena

Wynn Tamura

Peter Tarqueno

Jason Tavano

Helene Thibieroz

Hugh Thompson

Richard & Sandy Tompkins

Steve Tourdo

UCSB

USTA

Will Vail

Kristina Van Prooyen

Steve Velardi

Steve Vogt

Steve Ward

Scott Warner

Graham Weaver

Ben Wolfe

Tim Woodruff

Caryle Zipprich

About the Author

JEFF GREENWALD, MFT, is a licensed psychotherapist, best-selling author, and a leading expert in sports psychology, renowned for his book *The Best Tennis of Your Life*. A former number one world-ranked player on the ITF Masters Tour and professional tennis player, Jeff brings unparalleled experience both as a competitor and elite mental coach. For over twenty-seven years, he has empowered thousands of adult and youth athletes worldwide, helping them develop the mental edge and elevate their performance. As the founder of Mental Edge & Fearless Tennis (established in 1997), Jeff continues to shape the next generation of champions while competing globally on the Masters Tour. He was inducted into the Northern California Hall of Fame in 2019. Jeff is the father of two children, both of whom played multiple sports competitively over the past ten years. Visit him at mentaledgeforsports.com to learn more about the services he provides for athletes, parents, coaches, and corporate executives around the world.

www.ingramcontent.com/pod-product-compliance
Lightning Source LLC
Chambersburg PA
CBHW051618120626

46551CB00014B/1847